I will give you a Talisman.
Whenever you are in doubt,
or when the self becomes too much with you,
apply the following test:

"Recall the face of the poorest
and weakest man whom you may have seen
and ask yourself if the step you contemplate
is going to be any use to him."

Will he gain anything by it?
Will it restore him to a control
over his own life and destiny?
In other words, will it lead to Swaraj
for the hungry and spiritually starving millions?
Then you will find your doubts
and your self melting away.

—MAHATMA GANDHI

Faith and Interfaith in a Global Age

MARCUS BRAYBROOKE

Foreword by John Hick

CoNexus Press ~ GRAND RAPIDS
BRAYBROOKE PRESS ~ OXFORD

Published by
CoNexus Press
P.O. Box 6902, Grand Rapids, MI 49516 USA
tel. 616-452-1828 / fax 616-248-0943 / email: conexus@iserv.net
North American ISBN 0 9637897 2 4

and by
Braybrooke Press
Marsh Baldon Rectory
Oxford OX44 9LS United Kingdom
British ISBN 0 9516883 5 9

Printed in the USA.
Editing, design, and typesetting by Joel Beversluis.

$3/00$

Publisher's Cataloging-in-Publication
(Provided by Quality Books, Inc.)

Braybrooke, Marcus.
   Faith and interfaith in a global age / Marcus Braybrooke.
– 1st ed.
   p. cm.
   Includes bibliographical references.
   Preassigned LCCN: 97-78031
   ISBN: 0-9637897-2-4

   1. Religious pluralism. 2. Religions – Relations. 3.
Christianity and other religions. I. Title.

   BL410.B73 1998   291.1'72
                                    QBI97-41554

Contents

Preface

More and more people are waking up to the urgency and liberating excitement of interfaith activity. This book is intended to be a simple introduction to the history and issues of this growing, worldwide movement. The story begins with the World's Parliament of Religions in Chicago in 1893, but concentrates on developments since 1993, when the centenary of that event was celebrated in many parts of the world. Because I played a part in some of those celebrations and recent developments, this book also reflects my personal experiences, which, I hope, help make the book more readable and alive.

The book is also a tribute to my many friends and colleagues in the interfaith movement. I am particularly grateful to my wife Mary for sharing our interfaith journey, to Professor John Hick for writing a Foreword, to Sally Richmond for typing the book, and to Joel Beversluis for all his help in publishing this considerably revised version of what originally was issued as a booklet in 1995 under the title *Faith in a Global Age*. Some of the material here has appeared in articles and I am grateful to those who have given permission to reproduce it.

My hope and prayer is, in the words of Ven. Thich Nhat Hanh, that "all living beings realize that they are all brothers and sisters, all nourished from the same source of life."

Marcus Braybrooke
September 1997

Foreword

The impetus of the World's Parliament of Religions in Chicago in 1893 initiated a network of varied inter-religious organizations through which people of different faiths have been seeking to meet one another. Their aim has not been the missionary task of conversion, but, in a spirit of mutual respect, to engage in a many-sided and open-ended dialogue whose outcome lies in the unknown future. This network has grown, especially in recent decades; new movements and organizations are continually arising and new multifaith events are occuring all over the world. In this multifaceted phenomenon, no single person can have a complete picture of the changing worldwide situation.

However, Marcus Braybrooke probably has a wider experience of and participation in this activity, and a comparably greater knowledge of its literature, than anyone else in the Protestant ecclesiastical world. He has himself been a central figure at many focal points: he has been Executive Director of the Council of Christians and Jews, co-editor of the journal *World Faiths Insight* and is past Chairman and now Joint President of the World Congress of Faiths. He is an active figure in the rapidly developing International Interfaith Centre at Oxford, a Trustee of the Council for a Parliament of the World's Religions and of the Peace Council. He is a participant in the United Religions Initiative as well as a long-time supporter of the Temple of Understanding and Center for World Thanksgiving. He is the author of a number of books, including *Pilgrimage of Hope,* the definitive history of the first World's Parliament of Religions and of the various bodies that have continued in their different ways to embody its spirit during the succeeding century. He has been tireless in serving the cause of global inter-religious understanding, whilst being at the same time an active and faithful priest of the Church of England.

It is this wealth of knowledge and experience that make this new book so fascinating to read and such a valuable resource for those engaged in the search for interfaith understanding and for a new relationship between the religions of the world. It will attract the attention of all engaged in one aspect or another of the current discussions about religious plurality and the current growth of interfaith dialogue.

John Hick
May 1995

ONE

Introduction

I can still remember my surprise and excitement when I discovered Henry Barrow's record of *The World's Parliament of Religions* on a shelf of the Cambridge University Library.[1] It was to be twenty-five years before I was able to find and buy a copy from a second-hand bookseller. I had been looking for another book, but paused to browse and read some of the other titles. Here was an account of a gathering of members of different religions which took place in Chicago in 1893. At the time, in the late sixties, there were few other Anglicans who shared my interest in interfaith understanding. Within the churches there was a general assumption that Christianity was superior to all other religions. In any case, it was thought that as 'secular man' came of age, religions were losing their influence and knowledge of them was of little importance to Christians. In Barrow's book, however, I was in the company of others who believed in the cooperation of religions and who hoped that their respective insights were convergent.

It is only in the last few years as the centenary of the 1893 Parliament approached that there has been renewed interest in that amazing event.[2] For many years it was largely forgotten and another such gathering, held in 1933, was still not remembered in 1993.[3] When I came across Barrow's book, I did not know that I was to play a part in arranging some of the events held to mark the centenary of the Chicago Parliament. This most recent Parliament will also become a landmark event, so I want here, in the light of 30 years involvement, to reflect on how far the interfaith movement has come and on its future tasks.

That centenary has renewed interest in the World's Parliament of Religions and has given a new momentum to interfaith work across the world. Richard Hughes Seager, in his *The World's Parliament of Religions*, says the Parliament failed in its attempt to "forge a common religious discourse among representatives of both the religions of America and the world."[4] My central concern in this book is whether what was attempted but not achieved in 1893 has any greater hope of success more than one hundred years later. I am convinced that inter-religious understanding is a vital component of a more just and peaceful world order, but I also recognize how difficult it is to achieve.

The focus of this book is on the future, so it might be classified as one more contribution to the outpouring of "millennium literature." The reader may, however, find it easier to evaluate my suggestions if, first, I offer both a short autobiographical sketch and a summary of what has been attempted and achieved in interfaith work in the hundred years since the Parliament in Chicago.

* * * * *

When I happened upon Barrow's book, I was already Honorary Secretary of the World Congress of Faiths and was looking for a book about the relationship of Christianity to other religions. My interest in other religions began while I was at University. I attended a conference, organized by an Anglican Missionary Society, the United Society for the Propagation of the Gospel (USPG), at which the speakers included Bishop George Appleton, whose years in Burma inspired in him a deep reverence for the Buddha, Bishop Kenneth Cragg, a sympathetic student of Islam, and Dr. Basu, a Hindu who had studied European and Indian philosophy. Bishop Appleton spoke of "the Glad Encounter" of religions, while Dr. Basu spoke of the connections between the thought of Sri Aurobindo and of Teilhard de Chardin. All three speakers suggested that the meeting of religions was mutually enriching and could help to heal the divisions in the world. Together they shattered for me the arrogant assumption of many Christians that the Church has much to teach others and nothing to learn from them.

There was little opportunity at Cambridge University itself to learn about world religions. In my last term I attended, with four others, lectures by an Anglican pioneer in this field, A. C. Bouquet, who kindly spent some hours talking to me about his interests and his travels in India. These conversations were particularly helpful as I had been awarded a World Council of Churches scholarship to study Hinduism and Indian philosophy for a year at Madras Christian College (1962-63). I am very grateful for that experience, not least that my professor, Dr. C. T. K. Chari, who was himself a Hindu, had studied the philosophy of European science for his doctorate and was well versed in European as well as Indian thought. Further his brother had converted to Christianity, so Dr. Chari had deep insight into both religions. He arranged for me to visit and stay with several of his Brahmin friends in different parts of India.

On my return to Britain, I saw a small advertisement about the World Congress of Faiths (WCF); it was the reference to a library that attracted me, but I also went to a lecture by Professor Geoffrey Parrinder. This was at WCF's headquarters, which were then in Younghusband House in London. Soon after attending the lecture, I enrolled part-time to work for a higher degree under Geoffrey Parrinder. My thesis was a comparison of the developments in modern Hindu and modern Christian thought and was published as *Together to the Truth*. I was also soon asked to become a Joint Honorary Secretary of the World Congress of Faiths. All of this I had to fit into the life of a busy curate with two small children— it was only possible thanks to the understanding of my wife and my vicar.

The late sixties and seventies were as exciting a time in church life in Britain as in North America. New ideas, liturgical reform, and social concern were high on the agenda. Very slowly too the churches were waking up to the fact that Britain was becoming, at least in urban areas, multi-ethnic and multi-faith. This was a slow process and as late as 1980, Clifford Longley, religious correspondent for the *Times*, complained that the main denominations in Britain had taken hardly any interest in their neighbors of other faiths.[5] The same was true in other countries. It is hard to remember that the Inter Faith Network for the UK was established as recently as 1987 and the North American Interfaith Network (NAIN) in 1986.

Even so, in the late sixties and early seventies new questions were arising. For example, should churches allow Hindus or Sikhs to use their church halls for weddings or for worship? (Such halls were already used for dog training and bingo.) If a church was no longer required and made redundant, could the local Muslim community buy it and "convert" it into a mosque? If a special service was arranged for the United Nations Association, should members of all local faiths be asked to take part? In local schools, especially if a number of children were Muslim or Sikh or Hindu, should all the Religious Instruction be Christian? (British schools, unlike U. S. public schools, include instruction in religion.) Underlying these and other practical issues there was the theological question about the relationship of Christianity to other world religions. Some of my fellow Christian clergy looked askance at my belief that God was present in all the great communities of faith. They saw other religions as rivals, not partners. Whereas I, as quite often a Christian spokesperson for the WCF, took the other view.

My work for WCF was always on a voluntary basis and fitted into the commitments of my church work. In 1983, I was asked to become Director of the British Council of Christians and Jews (CCJ). This gave a particular form to my concern for dialogue, although I was concerned to help relate Christian-Jewish dialogue to the wider multi-religious dialogue. Even while at CCJ, however, I continued to co-edit, with Professor Seshagiri Rao, the journal *World Faiths Insight* (now called *World Faiths Encounter*) and to help build up WCF's links with other international interfaith organizations.

Gradually during the seventies, we at the World Congress of Faiths became aware of other bodies trying to do similar work;

these include the International Association for Religious Freedom (IARF), the Temple of Understanding (ToU), and the World Conference on Religion and Peace (WCRP). At the time the phrase "the peace movement" had become a common way to speak of the varied coalition of groups which opposed nuclear weapons. When in 1978 I became chairman of WCF, I started to speak of the "interfaith movement," to suggest that other groups were not rivals but that we all were part of something bigger. I also saw the need for these different groups to establish working relationships.

Eventually, in 1985, a meeting of international interfaith groups took place at the Ammerdown Conference Centre, near Bath. At this meeting one of the workshops expressed the hope that the various events which would be held to commemorate the 1893 Chicago World's Parliament of Religions might be linked and that the year "could provide an opportunity to touch people more widely with the spirit of interfaith dialogue."[6]

In 1988, for health reasons, I had to resign as Director of the Council of Christians and Jews. I have, however, continued to have responsibilities for congregations in Bath and now in Oxfordshire. I have also found time to write on Christian-Jewish and interfaith dialogue and to be involved in the centenary celebration of the Chicago Parliament and in subsequent developments, especially the establishment of an International Interfaith Centre in Oxford.

To prepare for 1993 an ad hoc International Interfaith Organizations Co-ordinating Committee (IIOCC) was set up to encourage worldwide observance of 1993 as a Year of Inter-religious Understanding and Cooperation.

None of the the four organizations had spare resources to devote to this project. Meetings of the coordinating committee were tacked on to other meetings to save air fares. The work of the secretaries, David and Celia Storey, and my own work as its chairperson was on a voluntary, unpaid basis. We had no office, but worked from our homes; the IARF undertook the enormous burden of the logistical arrangements for the 1993 inter-national conference in Bangalore.

Yet these very "disadvantages" were part of the excitement and significance of the Year. I had to learn that only what the Spirit owned would be of value and that the Spirit would provide the necessary resources. On one visit to India, I was met early in the morning at Delhi airport by Mary Pat Fisher, who took me to Gobind Sadan ashram. The remarkable guru, Baba Virsa Singh ji Maharaj, had promised to grant me an audience, so I did not dare go to sleep in case he sent for me. In fact, I waited most of the day, but would happily have waited longer to meet this inspiring holy man. His words were chastening. He insisted that only if those who prepared the conference were rooted in the Spirit would the event be of real value. There have been, as he knew and said, too many big gatherings of "religious leaders." To guide our planning throughout the time of prepa-ration for the Conference we kept the words of Gandhi's talisman by our front door.

> Recall the face of the poorest and
> weakest man whom you may have seen
> and ask yourself if the step you contemplate
> is going to be any use to him.[7]

Aware as I am of my failure to give enough time to prayer and meditation, I believe those of us engaged in planning the Year of Inter-religious Understanding and Cooperation did see it as a response to the Spirit's guidance, not to our planning. My first meeting with David and Celia Storey was unplanned and providential. At a vital moment, we were given a fax machine, without which the operation would have been impossible. At Bangalore itself, until the last moment we had difficulty in establishing a strong local committee. In the event, all the faith communities in Bangalore came together in a wonderful way. There were moments when it seemed that the whole enterprise of organizing a joint conference would collapse. The fact that it happened so successfully was indeed thanks to the Spirit.

In the midst of these times of testing, we were, I believe, learning about the nature of religious decision-making in a global society. Such decisions had to be by consensus; power could not rest in one place or one group or another would opt out. The emerging world society, in my view, also will be multi-centered, not dominated by one power or super-power. Modern communications do allow for international consultation. They also make it possible for people with very slender resources to influence world opinion. It is not necessary to wait for a multi-million dollar budget before action is possible nor is the mass media essential to the communication of ideas (although it is helpful). We relied on the mini media—the great number of newsletters and journals produced by religious groups. Thanks to my word processor, it was possible to adapt the same article to a Sikh or Muslim or Theosophist readership. In its very way of working, as well as in its concepts, the Year questioned many of the dominant assumptions of our contemporary society. The empowerment of "little" people is necessary for any spiritual renewal of world society.

As I look back, I think that the many public meetings and commemorations in 1993 have indeed heightened awareness of interfaith activity. This is one sign of the new, post-modern global society that is emerging, even if religious extremism also seems to be on the increase. A growing number of the designated leaders of all religions now recognize the importance of inter-religious understanding and cooperation and are seeking to justify it from their traditional sources. They are also emphasizing the moral values held in common and are at least pondering how religious people may act more effectively to meet the critical challenges to our world society. Yet important questions remain about how interfaith activity can be more effective in helping to create a better world. There are also questions about the philosophical and theological basis for interfaith cooperation, which tend to be glossed over.

My hope—though certainly not the hope of all in the interfaith movement—remains that dialogue will eventually bring convergence or, at least, that theology will become an inter-re-ligious discipline or "global theology." Even so, the meeting of religious people should not be just intellectual, but a sharing of the Spirit. Only such sharing will make possible the recovery of those spiritual values which offer hope to a world that is in agony. This book is a plea to all who are intrigued by or engaged in interfaith activity to try to discern the peaks we have yet to climb together.

TWO

The Interfaith Movement: Shaping the Present Reality

Hans Küng ends his book *Global Responsibility* with these words:

No human life together
without a world ethic for the nations.
No peace among the nations
without peace among the religions.
No peace among the religions
without dialogue among the religions.[1]

One hundred years ago, Charles Bonney, who presided at the World's Parliament of Religions in Chicago, ended his closing address like this: "Henceforth the religions of the world will make war, not on each other, but on the giant evils that afflict mankind." Sadly, religions have failed to fulfil that hope. Yet this century, for all its catastrophic wars and acts of genocide, has also seen the growth of a worldwide interfaith movement. Before trying to discern the path ahead, it is worth pausing to see what has been achieved. This is not the place to give a history of the interfaith movement, which I have attempted elsewhere. Rather I've described those several key factors that have shaped the reality as it was at the start of 1993, the centenary year of the World's Parliament of Religions. The events of 1993 and subsequent developments deserve a chapter to themselves.

The World's Parliament of Religions, Chicago, 1893

The World's Parliament of Religions was held as part of the World Fair or Columbian Exposition which marked the four hundredth anniversary of Columbus' "discovery" of America. The word "Parliament" was chosen to emphasize that participants of all religions were equal, but, in fact, the body had no executive or legislative authority. It reflected the optimism and self-confidence characteristic of the USA towards the end of the nineteenth century. Most of the participants were Christian from a wide spectrum of denominations. Their presuppositions permeated the gathering. Yet the contribution made by those of other faiths, although their number was small, was very significant.

The World's Parliament of Religions gave much attention to the contribution of religion to peace and social issues. Women were encouraged to play quite a part at the Parliament—more so than at most subsequent interfaith gatherings.

The Study of World Religions

The World's Parliament of Religions gave an impetus to the emerging study of world religions. While such study is an academic discipline in its own right, it has greatly increased awareness of the teachings and practices of world religions at every level. This century has seen an enormous increase in knowledge about world religions. Books, films, and videos are widely available. This study has helped to provide accurate information about the religions of the world. Even so, much ignorance and prejudice still exists.

Initially the study was confined to university departments devoted to the Science of Religions or the Comparative Study of Religions—although such departments were very unevenly spread across the world. Slowly, in some countries, the teaching of world religions has spread to schools, although the situation and law in every country is different.

For some time many scholars of the subject stood apart from the interfaith movement partly because they felt that their study should be objective or neutral and partly because they concentrated on the study of the texts and the history of religions. Now, in part because there is more interest in the faith and practice of believers, far more scholars take part in interfaith discussions; their participation has enriched the interfaith movement.

Knowledge may not of itself create sympathy. Opportunities for personal meeting and friendship are important to dispel prejudice and to encourage real understanding. Many interfaith groups attach much importance to providing opportunities for young people to meet. Often they discover that they face similar problems and that in every society many young people are questioning all religions. They may also discover how much people of all faiths can do together to work for a better world.

Organizations for Interfaith Understanding

No continuing organization emerged from the 1893 World's Parliament of Religions. At first slowly and recently more rapidly, interfaith groups have been established in many places. Some are quite small, meeting in a home. Members get to know each other and learn about each other's beliefs and practices. Sometimes members pray together or share in social or peace work. Other interfaith organizations are national bodies and some are international, seeking to coordinate global interfaith concern. By 1993, the established international interfaith organizations were the International Association for Religious Freedom, the World Congress of Faiths, the Temple of Understanding, and the World Conference on Religion and Peace.[2]

Those who take part in interfaith bodies seek for a bond between religious believers, despite the differences of belief and practice between and within the great religions. The interfaith organizations all reject "syncretism," which implies an artificial mixing of religions, and "indifferentism," which suggests that it does not matter what you believe. None of these organizations are trying to create one new world religion, although some other groups have that hope.

The interfaith organizations accept that most of their members will be loyal and committed members of a particular faith community. Respect for the integrity of other peoples' faith commitment and religious practices is essential. A few members of interfaith organizations may have no specific allegiance and describe themselves as seekers.

While aware of the distinctiveness of the world religions, members of interfaith organizations hope that some basis of unity exists or may be discovered, although the nature of the relationship of religions to each other is still much debated. For some people the unity rests upon our common humanity; for others there is an essential agreement between religions on moral values; for others there is a mystical unity, by which they mean that religious experience is ultimately the same and that differences are a matter of culture and language; others hope that through dialogue religions will come closer together and grow in their understanding of the Truth; others stress the need of religious people to work together for peace and justice and the relief of human suffering; for some, it is enough that there should be tolerance and respect, without bothering about questions of truth.

All these shades of opinion and many more are reflected within interfaith organizations, which have generally avoided trying to define the relationship of religions. For them, the search for understanding and cooperation is urgent in itself.

In their early years the international interfaith organizations tended to stress what united religious believers. Now, with greater trust and knowledge, equal emphasis is given to appreciating the distinctive contribution each faith—and the various traditions within each faith—make to human awareness of the Divine. Increasingly, those who occupy leadership roles in the various religious communities have begun to take an active part in interfaith organizations, whereas at first the initiative lay with inspired individuals. It has taken a long time to erode the traditional suspicion and competition between religions—and it still persists, especially in the problems created by aggressive missionary work. The main brake on the growth of interfaith understanding has been the conservatism of religious communities. Happily, now, those at the leadership level in many religious traditions recognize the vital importance of inter-religious cooperation.

Peace through Religion

While all efforts for interfaith understanding promote a climate of peace, some interfaith organizations, especially the World Conference on Religion and Peace, have concentrated on encouraging religious people to be active in peace work. Attempts to bring together people of different religions to promote peace date back to the early part of this century. Even so, the first Assembly of the World Conference on Religion and Peace did not meet until 1970. It is hard to assess the impact that religious people can have on political processes, especially as politicians seldom acknowledge those who have influenced them. Modern communications have given added weight to popular opinion.

Religious leaders may play an important role in forming public opinion by insisting on the relevance of spiritual and moral considerations. They have helped to maintain public alarm at the enormous stockpile of nuclear weapons and other means of mass destruction. They have voiced public outrage at the starvation of millions of people due to war, injustice, and unfair patterns of international trade. They have upheld human dignity and protested against torture and racism. They have underpinned efforts to develop internationally agreed standards of human rights and have helped to monitor their application. Interreligious conferences have been among the first to warn of threats to the environment. In local areas of conflict, religious people have often maintained contact across boundaries and divisions. Yet often, too, religious people have used religious loyalties to enflame conflict and have allowed particular interests to outweigh common human and religious moral values. Some extremists stir up religious passions to gain support for their own agendas.

It is even more difficult to evaluate the power of prayer, but certainly remarkable changes have recently taken place in the world scene, especially since the first World Day of Prayer for Peace at Assisi in 1986. Each year some people of all religions join in The Week of Prayer for World Peace. Special days of prayer are held to mark human rights anniversaries and for particular areas of conflict. Many people regularly repeat the Universal Prayer for Peace:

> Lead me from death to life, from falsehood to truth.
> Lead me from despair to hope, from fear to trust;
> Lead me from hate to love, from war to peace.
> Let peace fill our heart, our world, our universe.

Religious Institutions Engage in Dialogue

Often those who have pioneered the search for good relations between religions have faced misunderstanding and even hostility in their own faith community. They have been accused of compromising or watering-down the distinctive beliefs of their own religion. In fact, however, most pioneers witness that learning about other religions has helped them appreciate their own more deeply.

Slowly the value of interfaith dialogue has become more widely recognized. In the Christian world, in 1966, The Second Vatican Council's decree *Nostra Aetate* transformed the Catholic Church's attitude to people of other religions. A Secretariat for non-Christians was established, which is now called The Pontifical Council for Inter-Religious Dialogue. At much the same time, The World Council of Churches established a Unit for Dialogue with People of Living Faiths (now the Office on Inter-Religious Relations), which has arranged various consultations and has encouraged Protestant and Orthodox churches to rethink their theological approach to other religions.

Some other religions now have agencies to encourage dialogue; these include the International Jewish Committee on Inter-Religious Consultations and the World Muslim League's office for inter-religious affairs.

Clearly, official dialogue has a character of its own. Participants have some representative role. Much of the work is to remove misunderstanding and build up good relations, as well as encouraging practical cooperation on moral issues and social concerns. More speculative discussion about questions of "truth" may be inappropriate. Further, while most organizations fully respect the freedom of all who participate in consultations, the host organization may have its own agenda. This means that official inter-religious discussions need to be distinguished from interfaith organizations, where ultimate control rests with a board or executive which is itself inter-faith in composition and where funding comes from several religious communities. The growth of discussions between representatives of religious communities is, however, a sign that the importance of harmony between religions is now seen as urgent by the leaders and members of religious communities themselves. This is in part due to the pioneering work of interfaith organizations.

Bilateral Conversations

As in a family, there are times when the whole family wishes to be together and times when two members of the family want to talk by themselves, so there are times when members of just two religions wish to engage in dialogue. A particular example of this is Jewish-Christian dialogue. A major international organization, The International Council of Christians and Jews, was formed in 1975 to foster good relations between the two religions. Other examples are the growing Christian-Muslim dialogue, some Muslim-Jewish dialogue and considerable Christian-Buddhist dialogue both in North America and in Japan. There are now many study and conference centers in different parts of the world which promote dialogue between members of two or three religions.

The Practical Importance of Interfaith Understanding

The Gulf War, the Salman Rushdie affair, and the conflict in former Yugoslavia have emphasized the practical importance and urgency of interfaith understanding. No longer can anyone dismiss religion as obsolete or irrelevant to world affairs. But many wonder whether the future belongs to the interfaith movement or whether we are likely to see increasing religious rivalry. Some indeed have an apocalyptic vision of the next century being dominated by renewed conflict between Christendom and the world of Islam. The interfaith movement has serious problems to overcome if it is to achieve its goals.

In all religions there is an increase of extremism, which also alienates others from any religious allegiance. Missionary groups in some religions make exclusive claims that theirs is the only way to truth and salvation. Elsewhere religious differences enflame political and economic divisions and sometimes religion is exploited by the powerful as an instrument of social control. Even India, of whose tolerance Swami Vivekananda boasted at the World's Parliament of Religions one hundred years ago, has seen the increase of "communalism," or rivalry between different religious and ethnic groups.

In Eastern Europe, the renewed nationalism is often closely linked to religious identity and has been accompanied by anti-semitism and discrimination against religious minorities.

It is easy to deplore intolerance—especially in others. It is harder to understand its causes, which may be psychological or related to a group that is feeling politically, culturally, or economically marginalized. Intolerance may be caused by fear or ignorance or it may be based on exclusive claims to truth.

Even dialogue itself may be misused. As it becomes more popular, it may be "hi-jacked" for ideological purposes—that is to say, people may have hidden agendas such as wanting to change the views of their dialogue partners or seeking to gain their support for a political cause.

Much To Be Done

Despite all the problems, the interfaith movement has made progress, especially in recent years. Even so, it is still very weak.

The initiative was often with "marginal" groups—to whom all credit is due. Gradually liberal members of the major religions began to take part. Now, many religious leaders are committed to this work; even so, the religious communities are still reluctant to fund interfaith work, most of which is semi-voluntary. Cooperation between interfaith organizations is still only on an ad hoc basis. Adequate structures for greater coordination and cooperation are required. There is an urgent need, too, for centers of information about worldwide interfaith work. There is also much popular ignorance.

The Year of Interreligious Understanding and Cooperation in 1993 was intended to increase public awareness of the need for interfaith cooperation and to encourage those involved to assess their progress and to determine priorities for future work.

The educational task is still far from complete. The growth of comparative religious studies has helped to dispel ignorance about the world religions, but ignorance is still widespread. Theologians have helped their communities rethink traditional attitudes to other faiths, yet exclusive attitudes are still common. All religions claim insights into "Truth." There needs, therefore, to be continuing dialogue so that religions may share their insights and together come to a deeper understanding of Ultimate Reality. This dialogue includes both intellectual discussion and efforts to appreciate each other's patterns of prayer and meditation.

Yet in many cases the thinkers are quite remote from religious leaders. Meanwhile, religious rivalries destroy lives. Religious people are reluctant to make clear that their commitment to the search for truth and the defense of human rights is stronger than their group loyalty—costly as this may be.

The interfaith movement is becoming increasingly more practical with a new emphasis on ways of cooperating to face urgent problems and to seek a "global ethic" or consensus on moral values. The discovery of those who attended the first meeting of the World Conference on Religion and Peace in Kyoto, Japan, in 1970, was that "the things which unite us are

more important than the things which divide us." The interfaith organizations have shown that people of many religions
can agree on the importance of peace and justice and on action
to relieve suffering and to save the planet's eco-system.

The Year of Interreligious Understanding and Cooperation
in 1993 provided a chance to make the vital importance of
interfaith work far more widely known, not only in combating
extremism and communalism but in harnessing the energies of
all people of faith and of good will to tackle the urgent problems
of the world. Only by working together will the dreams of 1893
be realized. Only together will prejudice and discrimination be
removed, violence and injustice ended, poverty relieved, and
the planet preserved.

THREE

Globe-trotting

The best way to interest people in the Year of Inter-religious Understanding and Cooperation was to meet them and talk to them. Leading up to 1993, I took whatever opportunities I could to speak to groups in different parts of Britain and to attend international interfaith conferences. Even prior to 1988, I had been to gatherings of the Temple of Understanding, The World Conference on Religion and Peace (WCRP), and the International Association for Religious Freedom (IARF).

Every trip involved the problem of finding enough money. Sometimes the organizers would waive the registration fee, a number of trusts and individuals helped with air fares, and quite often Mary and I paid our own ways. The other difficulty was time, especially as I had responsibility for a congregation. Whenever possible, my wife Mary, who largely had to finance us both, came too, dedicating her holidays to interfaith work. The friendships made and the privilege of seeing different parts of the world far outweighed the pressures. More importantly, it made us ever more aware of the terrible difficulties and suffering of so many people's lives and also of the sacrificial dedication of thousands across the world who care for others and dream of and work for a better world.

I have hesitated whether to include some account of my travels here, yet the various conferences and the meetings with many people do provide the evidence on which subsequent ideas are based. Furthermore, I wish to pay tribute to those who are struggling for a new order to be born.

Energy for Change

The energy for change is enormous, expressed through small

27

inter-religious, peace, human rights, environmental, and welfare groups. It is these which convince me that a new world
order based on love and compassion is being born, although as
yet those who hold political and economic power seem scarcely
aware that such a new age is coming into being. President
Mikhail Gorbachev spoke honestly of this at the Global Forum
on Human Survival, held in Moscow in January 1990. He said
that new ideas begin with a creative and visionary few. Gradually their ideas spread and at a certain stage the media begin to
notice. When an idea becomes popular, politicians begin to act.
The longing for a new international order is beginning to
encourage politicians to speak about the environment or even
to intervene in defense of human rights. I believe that some of
the hopes and ideas which I express in this book reflect the
hopes of those in the interfaith movement who sense a coming
unity of the human family. To be effective, the need is for those
who share this vision to act together.

As we set out for India in 1993, a friend gave us a book to read
on the airplane. It began with these words, "Early this morning,
1 January 2021, three minutes after midnight, the last human
being to be born on earth was killed in a pub brawl in a suburb
of Buenos Aires, aged twenty-five years two months and twelve
days." As I said in my welcome to participants in the Bangalore
Sarva-Dharma-Sammelana,

> I believe there is an alternative. In preparations for this gath-
> ering we have been in touch with many people around the
> world who share this dream and work for it by their care for
> others, by their struggle for peace and justice and human
> rights, in their concern for the environment. The flowing
> together of so many streams of new life will create a river
> strong enough to wash away the stains of ethnic cleansing,
> racism, sexism, discrimination, communalism, and apartheid.
> Many people long for renewal, for a world rebuilt on spiritual
> principles. What is necessary is that those who share this hope
> should share their energies. The century which has seen cruel
> wars, appalling poverty, ghastly genocide, has seen also the

beginnings of a world society, with the establishment of the League of Nations and now the United Nations, with agreement about Human Rights, with new friendship between members of different faiths, with unprecedented international relief efforts and with many new international organizations.[1]

WCRP V

In 1989, we went to Australia for the Fifth Assembly of the World Conference on Religion and Peace, which was held in Melbourne. We had visited Australia once before because we have many relatives there. We quickly realized on this second visit that multi-culturalism had become an issue in Australia. The question of how people of many ethnic and religious backgrounds are to live together is as important in Australia as in Britain. There was also in Australia a growing sensitivity to the claims of the Aboriginals. The late Archbishop David Penman, who chaired the WCRP Assembly, even suggested that the date of Australia Day should be changed so as not to mark the arrival of the British fleet. I became aware in Australia how the traditional religions had until that time largely been left out of interfaith dialogue. Environmental concerns were also capturing public attention in Australia.

For me, the highlight of the conference was the morning vigil on Mornington Beach where participants of many faiths met in silence and then joined in the Third World Day of Prayer for Peace.

Immediately after the conference was the first planning meeting for the 1993 international centenary conference, including discussion of where it should be held. At the closing session of the 1893 World's Parliament, the proposal had been made that the next Parliament should be held in India in 1900. This had suggested India as a possible venue for the gathering. Neither IARF nor WCRP had held one of their world assemblies in India. India as a venue would ensure participation from almost every religion, which was important as we did not expect to find funds to pay travel costs of participants. As this commemorative meeting was to be an addition to the regular program of the four organizations, all of whose budgets were fully committed, this was relevant. It was also thought better to avoid New Delhi, which has so many international conferences, lest the distinctiveness of this conference be lost. August was thought to be the best month for many in Europe and America, but the fear was that it might be too hot. Bangalore was recommended for its climate and attractiveness and in the event proved to be an excellent venue.

On the way back from Australia, we stopped for two weeks in India, where we visited the Brahma Kumaris World Spiritual University in Mt. Abu and spent time in Delhi, where Fr. Albert Nambiaparambil kindly introduced us to many of the religious leaders.

IARF

The following year, 1990, it was the turn of the International Association for Religious Freedom to hold their Congress in Hamburg. My most vivid memories are not so much of the Congress as of the underside of rich European societies. The spartan hostel where we were staying was some way from the conference hall so we had to travel on the local underground. Late at night, the other passengers were either under the influence of drink or drugs. In the morning, mothers with their babies were begging for money. One evening we had a meal near our hostel. Outside the cafe was obviously the rendezvous for men to pick up prostitutes—yet another reminder of the degradation some people inflict on others. The most horrific reminder of this human cruelty was a visit to the site of a former concentration camp.

Hamburg made me more aware of the perilous alternatives to the attempt to build a tolerant society. The veneer of civilization is very thin and the dreams of which I have already written can so easily become a nightmare of ethnic cleansing or the alienation of an underclass. Yet the Congress itself affirmed the optimism and idealism of the International Association for

Religious Freedom, whose work ranges from conflict resolution in small, impoverished villages to consensus on religious freedom at the United Nations.

South Korea

In 1991, an unexpected telephone call invited me to a conference in South Korea. My hosts were the Won Buddhists. Their founder, Sot'aesan, who was born in 1891, had a vision of the essential unity of all religions. The conference was part of the celebrations of the centenary of his birth. It also was intended to see whether the international interfaith organizations could help effect contact between members of different religions in South and North Korea. At the time, no contact was allowed and I was made aware of the continuing and often very personal suffering caused by the division of Korea. Sometimes relatives had not seen each other for many years.

Just before setting out I was surprised by another telephone call, asking me to chair the conference and also to speak at the centenary celebration, which was attended by nearly thirty thousand people. When I arrived, I found that a delightful Korean Quaker was to help me in the task of chairing. The conference helped to build a continuing friendship with the Won Buddhists, who made a valuable contribution to the conference at Bangalore and who invited me back to their own 1993 celebrations.

Costa Rica

Another surprise was an invitation to a conference in Costa Rica, held partly in connection with the United Nations University for Peace. This was my first visit to Latin America, another area which is now beginning to take an active part in the interfaith movement. Here I was strongly reminded of the terrible suffering that followed the discovery of America by Columbus and the "Christianization" of the continent. It was good to talk, as best one could through interpreters, with some of the indigenous people. The interfaith movement has to ensure that those who are seldom heard in world society are given a voice. I was delighted that Goyo de la Cruz Cutimanco, from Costa Rica, was able to come to Bangalore, where he led a prayer, in Peruvian, at the opening ceremony.

Preparing for 1993

Some conferences were held as part of the preparation for 1993. In October 1991, The World Fellowship of Inter-Religious Councils, inspired and led by Fr. Albert Nambiaparambil, arranged a conference in Cochin. This was a great opportunity to meet with Indians who were involved in interfaith activity. It was followed by a preparatory visit to Bangalore. We gained considerable backing for our plans, but were also made aware of the continuing injustices suffered by the Dalits— some of whom felt that dialogue with high caste Hindus was in effect conniving in their sufferings.

Indeed some Protestants in India had come to feel that interfaith dialogue was irrelevant to their concern for social justice, although at the Bangalore conference some suggested that such a concern provides the basis for a liberation theology of dialogue.

In January 1992, I was invited to Delhi for a conference arranged by the Sikhs. This gave me an insight into some of the communal tensions in India, but also made me aware of the deep Sikh commitment to interfaith harmony. I made a further visit to Bangalore in February 1993, following a conference in Delhi, which was arranged by the Council for the World's Religions as their contribution to the Year of Inter-religious Understanding and Cooperation. The conference included an impressive march to the Red Fort as an act of witness to the unity of faiths in opposition to communalism and extremism.

The University of South Carolina

Appropriately, the first international conference to mark the centenary of the World's Parliament of Religions that Mary and I attended was at Columbia in South Carolina, USA. It was appropriate because the 1893 World's Parliament of Religions was held in connection with the World Columbian Exposition which celebrated the four hundredth anniversary of the "discovery of America" by Christopher Columbus. In fact, it was in October 1492 that Christopher Columbus reached the island of San Salvador. The four hundredth anniversary should have been in 1892, but it took time to decide the rival claims of several cities to host the Columbian Exposition. When a decision was eventually made, extra time was needed to mount the World Fair. Because of the link with Columbus, it was good to begin in a city named after him. The event was hosted by the University of South Carolina on the initiative of a long time friend, Professor Hal French, whom I first met at the headquarters of the Theosophical Society at Adyar, near Madras. The enthusiastic and warm support for the first big interfaith venture in the city was most encouraging. It was also good, on the final evening, to hear a memorable plea for interfaith cooperation from the charismatic African-American leader, the Rev. Dr. James Forbes of Riverside Church, New York. It was a reminder of just how wide is the backing for interfaith cooperation.

Berkeley

In the summer of 1992, it was the turn of San Francisco and Berkeley on the West Coast to host a centennial gathering. Much of the leadership was taken by Rev. Dick Boeke, an active member of IARF and at the time of Kensington Unitarian Church. This conference followed on from a meeting of the North American Interfaith Network (NAIN), so it provided the opportunity to share plans for 1993 with many of the leaders of interfaith dialogue in North America.

The Launch

The commemorations in 1993 began in January with the London Launch of the Year of Inter-religious Understanding and Cooperation. This was held at Global Cooperation House, by kind permission of the Brahma Kumaris, a spiritual movement founded in 1936 by Dada Lekh Raj (1877-1969), who is usually known as Brahma Baba. The committee, on which almost all faith communities in Britain were represented, had planned a day-long Launch.

Chaired by Lord Ennals, a former Labour cabinet member and a great worker for the United Nations, the day itself fell into three parts. The morning was more formal and included addresses by Lord Ennals and Dadi Janki, the Administrative Head of the Brahma Kumaris World Spiritual University, as well as by Bishop Trevor Huddleston, well known for his lifelong campaign against apartheid. Others included Dr. Mai Yamani, a social anthropologist from the Yemen; Swami Bhavyananda of the Ramakrishna Center; Rabbi Hugo Gryn, Vice-Chairman of the World Congress of Faiths; and Edgar D. Mitchell, the Apollo XIV astronaut. There was also a dramatic re-enactment of scenes from the 1893 Parliament. These contributions were punctuated by the water ceremony in which members of different faiths brought gifts of water to pour into a fountain and said a prayer. Christians brought water from the river Jordan, Muslims from Zamzam, and Hindus from the Ganges.

We spent the afternoon in workshops and the evening in a cultural program that included readings by Hayley Mills and John Cleese as well as music from different traditions. It was a long day, but inspired many local communities in Britain to plan interfaith events. The day also illustrated that the concern for good relations between different faith communities is not just of interest to 'religious' people, but is important to the whole community.

August 1993

The most exciting journey was to take us to centenary celebrations in India, Japan, and USA—all within three weeks in August 1993.

Kanyakumari

The first conference was at Kanyakumari, arranged by the World Fellowship of Interreligious Councils. Because of a delayed flight, we arrived there just a few minutes before I was due to speak.

The next day, appropriately, included a pilgrimage to Vivekananda's rock. Vivekananda, one of the great heroes of the 1893 Parliament, had spent Christmas 1892 at the rock, where he dedicated himself to the service of "My God, the poor, My God, the afflicted, My God, the down-trodden of all races." A small incident on the rock reminded us of the human fellowship at the heart of interfaith work. Perhaps not yet used to the heat, Mary felt quite unwell while we were on the rock. Several people offered to help. A Baha'i arranged for us to get straight back on the ferry. Then a Hindu drove us back to the hotel. An hour later there was a Zoroastrian lady at the door. She handed us an envelope. "Did you want this?" she asked. It contained our passports, tickets and some travellers checks. Yes, we did want it! We had discovered a caring which transcends all labels and boundaries.

Participants at Kanyakumari were from many parts of India, with a small number from other parts of the world. It was a relaxed, friendly occasion with plenty of time for worship and meditation.

Sarva-Dharma-Sammelana

Sarva-Dharma-Sammelana at Bangalore was an international gathering and the five-star Ashok hotel introduced us to an India with which we were unfamiliar. The hotel was most helpful and provided the necessary facilities for a large international gathering. It was feared that the price would be a deterrent for some people, especially Indian participants, but where necessary the registration fee was reduced or waived. Much of the conference took place in the hotel gardens, where special awnings had been erected.

The whole gathering was set in a context of prayer and

meditation. It began with a joyful and prayerful Opening Ceremony. This included the lighting of lamps, prayers of different faiths, a speech by the Governor, and a few other messages of welcome. It included a happy moment when participants greeted each other and wished one another peace. The final ceremony, arranged by the younger participants, was also a joyous and prayerful occasion. Each day, participants came together in the morning and evening, at the beginning and end of each day's program, for a time of prayer or meditation, led by members of a particular faith. In several cases, people of different traditions within a faith shared in the arrangements. The centrality of these times of prayer to the whole occasion was reflected in the fact that people arrived on time and that the leaders, respectful of other peoples' needs, observed the time constraints.

Much of each day was spent in one of three programs. The first was a carefully planned group exercise which produced Shared Ideal Visions of Interfaith Cooperation. A certain amount of preliminary work had been done for this program, but the hope that a number of groups around the world would have worked on the preparatory material and have submitted their ideas never really materialized. Even so, the intention was important because, if conferences are to bear their full fruit, many more people than those who can make long journeys need to be involved in the process.

The second program consisted of visits to local centers of prayer and worship. The hope was that the visitors would learn something of the spiritual paths of those who welcomed them. Many said that their hosts did indeed share deeply with them and gave them an insight into their interior life, which is difficult to discover from books. A poem read by one of the speakers caught the sense both of variety and unity:

God is one, but his names are many.
Religions are one, but its ways are many.
Spirituality is one, but religions are many.

Humanity is one, but human beings are many.[3]

The third program offered seven workshops: The Role of Religious Traditions in Rebuilding Communities Before, During, and After Conflict; Ethical and Spiritual Energies for Building Trust and Creating Conditions for Peace and Justice; Service and Solidarity; Education for Understanding; Towards a Shared World Ethic; and Inter-Religious Relations in the Future—My Vision.

Cultural programs were presented in the evenings, in some cases hosted by local communities. On the evening before the conference began, the local Brahma Kumaris hosted a dinner and an evening of talks and cultural events. Visitors also had a chance to see the Centre's museum. The following evening there was a memorable visit to the newly built Taralabalu Kendra, at the invitation of Dr. Shivamurthy Shivacharya Mahaswamiji. On another evening we watched a performance of "A Frog from the Sea," which included readings from the 1893 Parliament and which had first been performed at the UK Launch in January 1993. That same evening there was a beautiful display of Indian dance and a meal hosted by Center for World Thanksgiving of Dallas, USA, at which the 1993 Declaration of Thanksgiving was read for the first time.

On the final evening, the Bangalore committee hosted a delightful cultural program in which most of the city's faith communities took part. That evening perhaps most vividly expressed the appreciation, which was evident throughout *Sarva-Dharma-Sammelana*, of our religious and cultural diversity. So often difference is seen as a threat, whereas most of those who shared in the Bangalore gathering had a sense that this variety is in fact an enriching gift from God. The lasting memory is of the warmth of the friendship and of the wonderful experience of being "one family."

Delhi

From Bangalore, we led a group to visit Agra and made a

memorable stop at the world headquarters of the International Society for Krishna Consciousness at Vrindaban; then we went on to Delhi for a Day Centennial Meeting. The highlights were speeches from the Prime Minister of India Shri P.V. Narashima Rao and Dr. Karan Singh, President of the Temple of Understanding. The Prime Minister stressed that India's constitution gave equal respect to all faiths. After the troubles following the destruction of the mosque at Ayodhya, the various 1993 conferences were useful opportunities for the great majority who reject communalism to make their views clear. As Swami Dr. Shivamurthy had said in Bangalore,

> The need of the hour is not to construct or demolish the Masjid or Mandir. Instead, we should aim at demolishing the walls of hatred and enmity in the minds of Hindus and Muslims and learn to live in harmony as brothers and sisters of the same family on the firm foundations of mutual trust and friendship.[4]

Early in 1993, Delhi had been the scene of communal strife. It was very moving that on the last evening children of different faith communities presented a cultural program with songs and prayers from each tradition. I still can picture vividly the Zoroastrian children singing an evening prayer as Mary and I left to go to the airport for the flight to Japan.

Japan

In Tokyo, which was flooded by a typhoon, we were the guests of Risho Kosei Kai, a lay Buddhist organization. From there we traveled to Ise, where a day conference arranged by IARF Japan was held to mark the Centenary of the 1893 Parliament, at which I was asked to speak. Afterwards, it was moving to meet a Buddhist abbot whose predecessor, Shaku Soyen (the teacher of Dr. Suzuki, who did much to make Buddhism known in the West), had attended the 1893 Parliament. He showed us the medal that Shaku Soyen had been given in Chicago. The next day, participants in the conference were invited to take part in the ceremony for rebuilding the Ise Grand Shrine. It was a dramatic and generous break-through for members of other religions to be asked to share in this important Shinto ceremony. In the evening at the Tsubaki Grand Shrine, as guests of Rev. Yamamoto, we all took part in the *misogi* ritual.

Chicago

Reluctantly, we had to hurry away from the beauty of Tsubaki Grand Shrine to fly on to Chicago, where the Parliament of the World's Religions was already in full swing by the time we arrived. With some seven thousand participants it was at first rather overwhelming. The huge and varied program made it difficult to identify the most important events. Again there was great friendliness and always lively conversation as we waited for the crowded elevators. It was an amazing event and a credit to the Director, Dr. Daniel Gómez-Ibáñez, and all involved.

Many faith communities had been asked to present their own programs, so at times the Parliament felt like a religious market place. Yet several communities had brought outstanding people to participate in their programs. The Parliament was inclusive—even though the presence of Pagans led to a walk-out by some members of the Orthodox Churches. The participation of new religious groups was, however, an advance and helped me realize that it is wrong to try to predetermine where the Spirit is at work.

Major presentations at the Parliament drew attention to the pressing problems that face the world. Indeed, on the opening day, Dr. Gerald Barney of the Millennium Institute focused on the critical issues of our time. The Global Ethic, which I discuss more fully in Chapter Seven, was an attempt to respond to these. The procedure at the Assembly of Spiritual and Religious Leaders and for producing the Global Ethic may have been flawed, but it was significant that the focus of the Parliament was on the world and its problems, rather than on inter-religious relations. This showed that the interfaith movement had gone beyond dispelling prejudice and ignorance and persuading people of different faiths to meet. Now, the uppermost concern had become what the religions could do together to bring help and hope to a "world in agony." This concern for common action and the search for shared values is now at the top of the interfaith agenda.

As one of the Presidents of the Parliament, I was honored to be asked to offer one of the prayers at the final gathering, at which the main speaker was the Dalai Lama and at which the *Declaration Toward a Global Ethic* was read for the first time. There were many other moving moments during the week-long Parliament. I think particularly of listening to a Buddhist nun talk of her response when her life was threatened in a civil war. Like the Dalai Lama, she lived by the non-violence she professed.

Moving Home

Within three days of getting home, Mary and I moved house to Marsh Baldon Rectory, which is near Oxford—thus allowing us to help with the development of the International Interfaith Centre, which I describe in more detail in Chapter Eight.

Our three week trip to India, Japan, and the USA was a taste of living in a global society. For some politicians and business people such travel is a common experience. Millions of others have little chance to travel even within their own country. Yet the world that is coming is one in which modern transportation and communications will make both travel and contact easier and more international. How will this affect the religious life of this planet?

Korea and Japan again

Toward the end of 1993, I was invited by WCRP chapters to speak in Korea and Japan. I visited Hiroshima for the first time and was deeply moved by meeting and talking with a survivor. We made our way to the memorial for the victims of the Atom bomb, where we prayed together in silence. I recalled the words of the poet Elie Wiesel, a survivor of the Holocaust, who asked when he saw Hiroshima, "Am I looking at the past or the future?" I hope interfaith work can be a contribution to ensuring that the answer is that genocide and massive destruction belongs to a past that children of the next century will have outgrown for ever. If interfaith work is for the good of the world, it is above all for the sake of future generations.

* * * * *

Part of the point of mentioning these travels and events is to begin to demonstrate how widespread and varied is the attempt to create understanding and cooperation between members of many religions. Beyond these I've mentioned, there were and are numerous other inter-religious activities in which I did not participate; often they overlap with the work of peace or environmental groups or of charitable efforts to bring help and renewal to those who suffer. Although I am aware that many in all religions are untouched by the new ecumenical spirit and that forces of exploitation and oppression are deeply entrenched, the extent of this activity to create understanding and cooperation gives me hope that a new, more just and peaceful world order is in the making.

FOUR

A New Age

"The world today is on the verge of a new age and a new culture," wrote Father Bede Griffiths in one of his last books.[1] Other influential thinkers echo this sentiment, speaking of their expectations for the new millennium.[2] The belief that we are entering a radically new age in human history is more an intuition than a matter of argument. As yet, we cannot discern all of its features, but we can point to many significant changes which are taking place and which are sometimes called "a paradigm shift."[3]

As a child it was an exciting expedition to travel by bus some seven miles to the nearest town. Every time I enter an airplane, I wonder anew at the marvel of air travel. During my national service, I was posted for a time at Derna in North Africa, from where we occasionally tried to contact our headquarters at Benghazi by telephone. It was almost impossible to get a clear enough line on which to have any conversation. Now, one may speak to a relation in Australia and she sounds as if she is next door. Fax and e-mail reinforce the miracle. We are entering a global age. Even the poor who do not share the opportunities of this new age can find their livelihood decimated by decisions on a distant stock market. Multinational companies are becoming global companies. Satellite communications are making possible global media networks. We need to think globally, even if we still need to act locally. This of itself should transform our thinking and lead us to question old boundaries.

Indeed this may be why the idea of a Global Ethic has aroused some hostility. I introduced a discussion of it to a group of Christian, Jewish and Muslim scholars and was surprised that some reacted very negatively to the concept. I had expected criticisms of the procedure or actual wording. Only afterwards did I begin to reflect that perhaps the hostility was an unconscious reaction to the global society that a global ethic assumes. For in a global society, traditional boundaries between faith communities and nations are relativized. Much interfaith dialogue encourages mutual understanding and appreciation, but shies away from questions of truth. Just as nations like to assert their sovereignty and resist outside interference, so faith communities may be resistant to any suggestion that there is a global ethical norm by which their particular ethical teaching may be judged.

Yet the grave issues that face our world are global issues. Ecological damage in one place can affect a whole continent, as was discovered after the accident at Chernobyl. The poverty of millions in Africa is partly caused by unfair world trade, while many wars are fueled by arms supplies which help to make rich nations richer. Too few politicians, dependent on national electorates, dare think in global terms. Religious communities are often just as parochial. Living in a world society should challenge many of the ways we think.

Other changes also suggest that we are entering a new and uncharted world. Three books have made me more aware of this. There are new approaches to science, some of which are summarized by Bede Griffiths in his *A New Vision of Reality*. There are changes in our ways of thinking, clearly described by Leonard Swidler in his *The Meaning of Life at the Edge of the Third Millennium*. And there are political, economic, and social changes which Hans Küng cites as evidence of a "paradigm shift" in his *Global Responsibility*.

Moving away from a Mechanistic Model of the Universe

Fr. Bede Griffiths, a Benedictine monk who settled in India in the fifties and who in 1968 moved to the Saccidananda Ashram by the sacred river Cauvery in south India, sought to discover the spiritual meeting point of Christianity and Hinduism. He was interested in a wide range of subjects and, in *A New Vision of Reality*, indicates how some scientists are putting forward radically new understandings of the world. The age that began with the discoveries of Galileo and Newton, he says, led to the gradual development of a materialist philosophy and a mechanistic model of the universe. The sciences, including physics, have been based on a mechanistic view of the world. This has affected our whole view of life and underlies the industrial system and modern technology.

Some recent philosophers and scientists are now questioning this underlying world view. Some have suggested that the material universe is essentially a field of energies in which parts can only be understood in relation to the whole and that the whole is in some way present in every part. As Griffiths says, referring especially to the writings of David Bohm, "we are living in a universe which is coordinated and integrated as a whole."[4] It is easy to see how this is reflected in concern for the environment and the talk about ecosystems.

The biologist Rupert Sheldrake has questioned the attempts to explain life in terms of physics and chemistry alone. His thesis is that "although there are fields of energy in the universe, the universe cannot be explained in terms of energy alone; there has also to be a formative power."[5] In differentiating his position from a mechanistic one, Sheldrake uses the analogy of a radio.

> The radio is a mechanistic system and it has to be in working order, but when the mechanism is correctly set up it works by being tuned into events from outside. The materialistic view would be that everything can be explained in terms of the mechanism of the radio.[6]

Such a view is reflected in the change from a mechanistic view of medicine to a recognition of the relation of the physical to the whole human person.

Griffiths also refers to developments in psychology, arguing that in Western psychology everything is referred to the ego, the centre of the individual self, and life is lived as if there is nothing beyond that. . . . This is precisely where the East has gone far beyond the West and has developed the understanding and experience of transpersonal consciousness.[7]

Ancient cultures integrated the physical, psychological, and spiritual, but this was lost at the time of the Renaissance. Griffiths points too to the fact that in most ages art was related to the sacred, with the sense of a sacred vision.

As the cosmic vision of the new science and philosophy takes over we may hope that there will be a renewal of art, not merely in the sense of the fine arts, but in all the humble daily expressions of a sense of beauty, which is also a sense of the sacred in human life.[8]

Ancient cultures were also aware that ultimate truth transcended human understanding and our intimations of the ultimate were most adequately expressed in myth and symbol.

We recognise today that myth is the most adequate way of expressing what cannot be properly expressed in human language. The ultimate state of humanity and the universe cannot be properly conceived, since it must transcend our present mode of consciousness. Myth or symbolic language is the only way in which the ultimate truth can be presented. Even the language of science is essentially symbolic.[9]

With these changes in mind, Bede Griffiths sought to discern the pattern of a new age.

It will be a human society based on a new relationship to the world of nature, arising from an organic understanding of nature in place of a mechanistic view of the universe. . . . We have to see ourselves as part of the physical organism of the universe. We need to develop the sense of the cosmic whole and of a way of relating to the world around us as a living being which sustains and nourishes us and for which we have a responsibility. . . . This would involve a new attitude to the earth and all living beings.[10]

Secondly, he writes, "the sense of communion with an encompassing reality will replace the attempt to dominate the world."[11] "Thirdly, these new values would give rise to a new type of human community."[12]

Griffiths speaks also of humankind's spiritual future, picturing the emergence of a cosmic universal religion, in which the essential values of the Christian religion will be preserved in living relationship with other religious traditions of the world. We shall return to Griffiths' vision in the final chapter. At times, to my mind, he shows a nostalgia for an idealized past. While the new age will be a critique of the modern world, it should not be and I think cannot be a retreat to the past. Rather it will be a new response to a new world, even if one deeply indebted to the past. Nonetheless, Father Bede Griffiths articulates many features of the emerging new age and has pioneered the *marriage of east and west*, to use the title of one of his books.[13]

A New Understanding of Knowledge

There is also a significant shift in our understanding of knowledge. Leonard Swidler, in *The Meaning of Life at the Edge of the Third Millennium*, says that our understanding of truth statements has been "deabsolutized."[14] We recognize that all statements about reality are conditioned by their author's historical setting, intention, culture, class and sex. Further we recognize the limits of language and that all knowledge is interpreted knowledge. Reality speaks to each person with the language he or she gives it. We are not in the position to make ultimate, unconditioned statements. This is why the renewal of symbols and the use of the imagination is so important.

Before the nineteenth century in Europe, Swidler writes, *truth*—a statement about reality—was conceived in an absolute, static, exclusivistic, either-or manner. If an assertion was true at one time, it was true for all time. In the nineteenth century scholars came to see that all statements were partially products of their historical circumstances and could only be fully understood if placed in their historical situation, their *sitz im leben*. Statements, therefore, were seen to be de-absolutized, that is limited in terms of time.

Secondly, it was recognized that we ask questions so as to obtain knowledge or truth. The questions we ask and how we pose them partly determine the shape of the answers we arrive at. This intentional view of truth also de-absolutizes statements because they have to be understood in relation to the thinker. Then, early this century, Karl Mannheim pointed out that all reality is perceived and spoken of from a cultural, class, and sexual perspective. Every statement is from a particular point of view.

Later in this century, Ludwig Wittgenstein and many others observed the limitations of language. Every description of reality is only partial, because although reality may be observed from many perspectives, language can express things from only one perspective at a time. Truth is limited by language. This is especially the case in language about the Transcendent. Further, the discipline of hermeneutics stresses that all knowledge is interpreted knowledge. That is to say in all knowledge it is "I" who comes to know something. This is the so-called interpretative view of truth. Indeed reality can only "speak" in the language that I give it. This dialogic view of truth implies that if our answers are confused or unsatisfactory it is because we are failing to distinguish different sorts of truth—for example, trying to understand living things in mechanical categories.

Our growing awareness of how we think has changed many of the ways in which we look at the world. In terms of our religious understanding, these changes imply a historicizing and de-absolutizing of religious statements. That is to say, no creedal or doctrinal statement has absolute and permanent truth. Any such statement is the product of particular people who lived at a particular moment in history. The great truths of religions have a symbolic value. Absolute claims to religious truth fail to recognize the limitations of human knowledge. The mystics of all faiths have said that the Mystery of the Ultimate transcends our understanding. *Neti, neti,* "Not this, not that."

This is a position rejected by the so-called "fundamentalists" of all faiths, who claim an unchanging and absolute authority for their beliefs. Their way of thinking does not allow for other truths. This means that they also reject the notion of a pluralistic society. Those who hold other views cannot be granted the same status as those who possess the truth.

The basic presuppositions of the pluralist interfaith position and of the fundamentalist position are opposed to each other. This is why it is worth trying to understand the presuppositions of those who speak of a new age and an emerging pluralist world society. It is the vision of a society based on mutual understanding, cooperation, and interdependence. The fundamentalist option leads to confrontation and conflict.

The Post-modern Paradigm

Professor Hans Küng has also spoken of a post-modern world and sought to characterize it. In his *Global Responsibility,* he talks of a "paradigm" shift from modernity to post-modernity, which he argues began to happen around the time of the First World War with the collapse of bourgeois society and the Eurocentric world.[15]

The paradigm theory is associated with Thomas Kuhn, who suggested that a basic model or paradigm was accepted in the scientific community until challenged by new data and ideas.

Hans Küng has suggested that in the same way there are at different periods of history different basic assumptions. In *Global Responsibility* he tries to identify the "dimensions of the overall constellation of postmodernity."

1. Geopolitically, we have a post-Eurocentric constellation: the domination of the world by five rival European national states (England, France, Austria, Prussia/Germany and Russia) is over. Today we are confronted with a polycentric constellation of different regions of the world, with North

America, Soviet Russia, the European community in the lead, and later probably also China and India. [This was written in 1990 and is already dated, for example, in the reference to the Soviet Union. The omission of Japan is surprising].

2. Foreign policy has to reckon with a post-colonial and post-imperial world society. Specifically (in the ideal case) this means nations which cooperate internationally and are truly united.

3. Economic policy has to reckon with the development of a post-capitalist, post-socialist economy. With some justification it can be called an eco-social market economy.

4. Social policy has to recognize the increasing formation of a post-capitalist, post-socialist society. In the developed countries it will be increasingly a society dominated by service industries and communication.

5. Those concerned with sexual equality see the appearance of a post-patriarchal society. In family, professional, and public life a relationship is clearly developing between men and women which is more of a partnership.

6. Culturally, we are moving in the direction of a post-ideological culture. In the future it will be a culture more orientated on an overall plurality.

7. In religious terms, a post-confessional and inter-religious world is coming into being. In other words, slowly and laboriously a multi-confessional, ecumenical world society is coming into being.[16]

Küng argues, in a way that is similar to Bede Griffiths, that the paradigm shift is not anti-science but that it de-absolutizes science and encourages a holistic view. The shift is also not anti-modern. Küng rejects anti-Enlightenment views and the views of those who would return to a "Christian Europe," affirming that post-modernity transcends and replaces modernity. Küng also rejects the argument that post-modernity is equivalent to radical pluralism and relativism. He insists, however, that there can be no uniform interpretation of the world in which we live.

Küng claims that this paradigm shift does not include a destruction of values, but rather a fundamental shift:

> from an ethic-free society to an ethically-responsible society; from a technocracy which dominates people to a technology which serves the humanity of men and women; from an industry which destroys the environment to an industry which furthers the true interests and needs of men and women in accord with nature; from the legal form of democracy to a democracy which is lived out and in which freedom and justice are reconciled.[17]

Even within the new paradigm there will be a multiplicity of heterogeneous options for living, patterns of action, language games, forms of life, scientific conceptions, economic systems, social models and communities of faith, but these do not rule out a fundamental social consensus.[18]

The Declaration *Toward a Global Ethic*, drafted by Hans Küng, which we shall discuss in Chapter Seven, is an attempt to articulate such a fundamental social and moral consensus.

Pluralism or Fundamentalism

To recognize the limits to religious claims to truth makes possible the acknowledgement of authentic apprehension of the Divine in other faith communities besides one's own. This is not possible for the fundamentalist who does not accept the views of truth outlined above. Küng has applied the paradigm theory to religious history and has suggested that there are basic assumptions which underlie religious thought, but that these assumptions change over the course of history. Thus even in the same religion there are in time radical shifts in basic world views. Fundamentalists, however, adopt an a-historical attitude to the central "truths" of a religion. They are unchanging and not open to reinterpretation in a changing world. Likewise, fundamentalists reject the idea of symbolism regarding their own truths—they take their particular myth as true in a literal sense. As Niels C. Nielsen argues in his *Fundamentalism, Mythos and World Religions*, "fundamentalists do not demythologize."[19] Nielsen argues that the failure to understand the nature of myth and to recognize that all "truth" is historically conditioned is characteristic of fundamentalists in all religions.

For the fundamentalist, there is only one truth—which they possess. They cannot then accept a pluralist society in which equal status is given to a variety of truth claims. They are committed, by the logic of their belief, to work for the victory of their views. Many do so by honest democratic persuasion, but others seek to coerce their opponents.

The pluralistic interfaith vision rests on radically different presuppositions. It assumes the possibility of those of different faiths respecting each other and affirming together certain basic moral values. It opens out also the possibility of theology becoming an inter-religious discipline and also the possibility of people of one faith absorbing into their spiritual life practices from another faith.

In my view, the interfaith vision is in tune with the character of the emerging post-modern global society. Indeed it offers the hope of a world civilization based on spiritual values, whereas the fundamentalist approach is likely only to lead to confrontation and conflict. This is why an understanding of the choice is so vital.

The Signs of a New Age

The new age is one in which lines of demarcation are blurred. Insights into the physical universe suggest that the part must be understood in relation to the whole. Medicine treats the whole person. Economies of nations become intertwined. Problems of poverty and environment are global. We begin to discern how in the ecosystem all life is woven together. We recognize that all knowledge is relative to the knower and that our growth in knowledge depends on sharing the knowledge of others.

My picture then of an emerging world society is one in which our interdependence is acknowledged and in which society is shaped by cooperation. We need to learn to live in harmony with nature, to respect it and not to exploit it. We need to learn to share so that no one goes hungry or homeless. We need to discover how people of different races, cultures and religions can live together creatively in society so that each person's contribution is acknowledged and no group dominates or discriminates against others. Modern technology, rightly used, allows people to participate in determining their future. A far more genuinely democratic society and world is possible.

Is this just a dream, and might we retreat behind old barriers and reinforce them? Communalism in India, ethnic cleansing in Eastern Europe, tribalism in Africa, fascism, and religious extremism are all denials of the future and are life threatening. Is it possible that the great world faiths together can help us all discover the abundant life which, I believe, God wills us to enjoy? The slogan "Dialogue or death" has the ring of truth.

If the great faiths are, however, to help shape a new world society based on love and compassion, they have first to repent of their long histories of ignorance and hostility.

FIVE

Repentance

The Abuse of Religion

"I am ashamed of my religion," said the fourteen year-old Protestant Gillian Burns. Her father had just been shot dead in the slaughter at the Rising Sun pub at Greysteel, Northern Ireland. Her father, the only Protestant among the seven victims, was killed when two Protestant gunmen sprayed the bar's customers with automatic gunfire. It was a "revenge" killing for the murder of Protestants by Catholics during the previous week.[1]

This grim headline reminded me of another, which appeared early in 1993. It read, "The little Bosnian girl whose mistake was to be a Muslim." The article told how three year-old Samira had been abused by Serbian soldiers. The mother, called by the soldiers a "Muslim bitch," had herself been raped.

When the mother found her daughter the girl was unconscious. Yet it was another Serbian soldier (the only good *chetnik*) who helped her at this moment. He bathed the girl under a cold water tap and that night crept into the prison room with a hard boiled egg and bread for the girl. He said if he found the soldier who had committed the outrage, he would kill him with his own hands.[2]

Even as religion is misused as a cloak for cruel and obscene acts, the protest against this misuse is also in the name of religion. The Year of Inter-religious Understanding and Cooperation was also marked by ethnic cleansing in Bosnia and began with communal violence in India. This gave to all the commemorative events a note of modesty and penitence. I soon learned that in India it was better to speak of a "spiritual" conference, because the word "religion" had negative overtones for many people.

Cruel acts have been perpetrated in the name of religion in every century and on every continent. Often religious people distance themselves from such abuse of religion. But the sense of being "saved" or "chosen" or "liberated" is a characteristic of many religious communities and may, perhaps unintentionally, be a cause of prejudicial attitudes to others.

Even the tolerant may be very intolerant of intolerance. It is tempting for "we tolerant liberals" to distance ourselves from the misuse of religion by blaming extremists. But this is to evade the call to repentance and the need to accept responsibility for the acts of our community, even if we disapprove of those acts.

The Need for Repentance

Dr. Jonathan Sacks, the Chief Rabbi of the British Commonwealth, in speaking of the need for repentance has pointed out that at the Jewish Passover ten drops of wine are spilled as a reminder of the sufferings of the Egyptians. The story of each faith community has its "enemy figures." The stories of English martyrs recall, for example, oppression by Protestant rulers in England, while the heroism of Sikh gurus was in the face of Muslim hostility. The negative image of the other is present in many traditions.

Christians now recognize with penitence that for centuries they have "diabolized" the Jews. Much Mediaeval literature about the Jews was obscene. Christian heretics did not fare much better. Christian-Muslim relations are still scarred by memories of the Crusades.

Europeans need to acknowledge the horrors of the slave trade and of colonialism. The 1893 World's Parliament of Religions was linked to the Columbian Exposition held to mark the 400th anniversary of the "discovery" of America by Columbus. A century ago the link was no problem, but now it has at times been an embarrassment. The Christianization of the Americas, which followed the so-called discovery of America, was accompanied by much cruelty.

At the conference in Costa Rica, I began to recognize the extent of this pain. There was a chance to meet with some of the indigenous people of Latin America, as well as to listen to a Liberation Theologian. By the end of his lecture I saw that I embodied the oppressor. I was white, male, Anglo-Saxon, and Christian. I said this to the lecturer afterwards and we laughed. We cannot escape the burden of our inheritance, but by acknowledging it, we can help to ensure that it does not cast a shadow on future generations.

A religious community shows its integrity by the honesty of its self-criticism. Even if confession is a regular part of the services, it is easy for religious institutions to become self-defensive under criticism. The new relationship between Jews and Christians has only been made possible by Christians honestly admitting centuries of anti-Jewish teaching in the churches and by trying to purge their teachings and liturgies of all that is anti-Jewish.

Yet prejudice is found not only in explicitly libellous comments, but in imagery and patterns of thought. Too easily Christians have applied metaphors of war to the spiritual life. They have felt encircled by the troops of Midian, who "prowl and prowl around." The hymn continues:

> Christian, up and smite them,
> Counting gain but loss;
> Smite them by the merit
> Of the holy Cross.[3]

The image of a chosen community has suggested that people of other races and religions are shut out from God's love. Men have assumed lordship over women. Anthropcentrism has denied humanity's oneness with the animal and natural creation.

It is not just a matter of imagery. Christians have often conceived salvation history as the struggle of good against evil and regarded their opponents as the forces of evil. Is evil to be destroyed or redeemed? There is an alternative Christian vision of reconciliation in which we recognize the shadow that is part of each one of us and see wholeness not as its suppression, but as its integration. It is a vision of love which in the end wins to itself that which is evil, not by destruction but by inner change.

I believe, as I wrote in *Dialogue with a Difference*,[4] that our vision of God, our picture of Ultimate Reality, matters profoundly. Writing during the Gulf War, Tony Higton, an outspoken conservative evangelical Anglican clergyman, said, "I suspect some of the anti-war idealism is related to the widespread modern reaction against discipline and punishment." His emphasis on punishment is based on his view of the way God deals with sinful men. In his book, *What is the New Age?*, he writes, "Without a terrible death-penalty (inflicted on Christ), God's just law could not be satisfied and mankind saved."[5] If, however, we picture God as a mother comforting us in our sorrow, our hope will be that any punishment is remedial and we shall believe that God's power is in the force of suffering love.

I shall not develop this now, but I believe the task of purging our religious thought of xenophobia and the enemy-image requires deep theological reflection. What is our picture of God? Mine is of a God whom Jesus Christ has shown to be of unconditional, vulnerable, accepting love. A God who loves all creatures so deeply that God will never cease to love them so that all may reach fulfilment. To those who thus picture God, the way of self-giving, sacrificial, non-violent love is integral to the Gospel. Such a God has no favorites. The God whom I see revealed in Jesus Christ is a God who loves all people. In our meeting with those of other faiths we shall expect to learn more of the wonderful ways God deals with men and women.

Other faiths also have a need for purification so that the central experience of the Transcendent cleanses and regenerates each community of faith. Where that happens there will be the desire for penitence and reconciliation with those of other faiths. There will be a willingness to admit that a religious tradition has been misused and should not be a cause of human division.

Many Christians now recognize that centuries of anti-Jewish teaching prepared the way for the horrors of the Holocaust. In recent years, some public acts of penitence and reconciliation have taken place. For example, the Pope's visit to the Rome synagogue in 1986 was described as his longest journey, crossing nearly two thousand years of history. North American Lutherans have repented of their theological complicity in the Holocaust.

In Britain, as an act of reconciliation, the world premiere of the musical work "Kaddish for Terezim," which included some of the poems written by the children who were imprisoned in the Terezim concentration camp, was held in Canterbury Cathedral, before a mixed Christian-Jewish audience. In 1989, services of reconciliation were held in York to remember the massacre of Jews there at Clifford's Tower in 1189. History can cast a long shadow.

Some years ago, the new Japanese Buddhist movement, Rissho Kosei Kai, sent a group of young members to neighboring Asian countries to apologize for Japanese behavior during the war. In November 1993, the Japanese Prime Minister, during a visit to South Korea, came close to apologizing for Japanese behaviour during World War II.

Bishop Desmond Tutu, writing in 1991, stressed the need for the perpetrators of apartheid to apologize if there was to be any lancing of the poison.

> I have no doubt that repentance and forgiveness are indispensable for setting right relationships between those who have been wronged and wrongdoers within nations and between nations. Unless you deal with the past in a creative and positive manner then you run the terrible risk of having no future worth speaking about. The past can have a baleful or beneficent impact on the future. [Hopes for a new democratic South Africa] will be seriously undermined if those who benefited from the obnoxious apartheid system, perceived as

the oppressors, will not ask for forgiveness for the awful things done under apartheid and if the victims, the oppressed, do not offer forgiveness.[6]

I have labored the point about repentance because I do not believe that people of faith can work together until they acknowledge and seek pardon for the painful past. That means saying "I am sorry!" to members of other faiths and to those of no faith who have been wounded by religious intolerance. It also requires purging religious traditions of anything that bears false witness about others and of the arrogance that would limit the love of God to a particular religious community. Only as religious people seek mutual forgiveness of past misunderstanding and bitterness will they have the strength to stand together and reject the interpretations of the extremists. Only then can religious people speak as the "moral conscience of humankind."[7]

This awareness of religions' checkered history was expressed at the Opening Ceremony of *Sarva-Daharma-Sammelana* at Bangalore. A responsive reading included these words:

Leader: We come together confessing that often we have failed to live by the teachings of our traditions which urge care of the earth, respect for others and justice for all.

People: We come in confession.

Leader: We come together with awareness of the harsh conflicts in the world, of the religious hatred that scars the hearts of many, and of the suffering of those who are less fortunate than we.

People: We come in awareness.[8]

At the closing ceremony of the 1993 Parliament of the World's Religions, the introduction to the "Declaration Toward a Global Ethic" was read. It included these words: "In particular we condemn aggression and hatred in the name of religion."[9]

The Dangers of Religious Extremism

The search for interreligious understanding and cooperation has both to seek healing for the past and to struggle against the misuse of religion by extremists who use religious differences to aggravate existing divisions and conflict.

It is paradoxical that the interfaith movement which seeks cooperation between religions is itself a cause of division. Many who have been involved in interfaith work have said that while they make friends of members of other religions they become enemies to some members of their own religion. There are some Christians, for example, who see interfaith work as a betrayal of the unique claims of Jesus Christ.

It is important to avoid labeling all critics of interfaith work as extremists or fundamentalists. There are those who have genuine fears that interfaith dialogue may weaken the commitment of members of their faith community. They worry too that the study of religions may lead to a certain detachment from any particular faith.

The term "fundamentalist" may also be misleading. It was first used of Protestants in the USA who, in reaction to evolutionary theories and Biblical criticism, insisted on the verbal inerrancy of scripture. In that sense it would be true to say that almost all Muslims are "fundamentalist" in their view of the Qur'an, but this would ignore the variety of legal interpretations within Islam. There is in fact considerable variety in Islam, and the great majority are not extremist.

I doubt whether the use of the word "fundamentalist" of movements in different religions is particularly helpful. Niels Nielsen, however, in his *Fundamentalism, Mythos and World Religions,* suggests that there are common characteristics among those who may be called fundamentalist in different religions.[10] All are convinced that their beliefs are true in a literal sense, and they have no place for the truths that others hold dear.

Nielsen suggests that theological interpretation arises out of a commitment to an underlying symbolism. Each major relig-

ion has its own distinctive symbolism or *mythos*. Fundamentalists in each religion, he argues, take that *mythos* as true in a literal
sense. They do not "demythologize." Equally, fundamentalists
do not accept that the central truths of a religion are subject to
historical change. Some Christians, for example, speak of "the
faith once delivered to the apostles." A non-fundamentalist, by
contrast, recognizes that these truths are historically conditioned; that is to say, how they are expressed reflects the way of
thinking of those who voiced them and that therefore they need
to be re-expressed in the language of succeeding generations.
Fundamentalists, Nielsen says, claim a literal belief in the truths
of their religion, which are unchanging and not subject to
re-interpretation with the passing of time. Fundamentalists
reject the de-absolutizing of truth which, it was suggested in the
last chapter, is a characteristic of the emerging post-modern and
global age.

Pluralist Societies

Such a view allows for no alternative approaches to the truth.
Truth is single. The political danger is that if fundamentalists
gain power, they allow no place in society to those with other
beliefs. This is why those who are committed to interreligious
cooperation and who have a pluralist view of society are bound
to find themselves in opposition to fundamentalists. Part of the
difficulty, however, is that many who are not fundamentalist
still work on assumptions which were relevant when a society
was shaped by a particular religious tradition but which are no
longer relevant today.

In Britain, for example, in 1988, an Education Reform Bill
was debated in the House of Lords. During the debate a number
of peers spoke of Britain being a "basically Christian country"
and argued for the preeminence of Christianity in the schools'
Religious Education. Lord Beloff, who is a Jew, expressed the
apprehension this caused to those who belonged to minority
religions. "Such a person like myself," he said, "and people who

believed themselves to be part of this nation, although practicing different faiths, are somehow second class citizens."[11]

In Eastern Europe, the reassertion of national identity has often made religious minorities uneasy. They are not felt to be part of the new nation.

In India too there are those who would like the country to be a Hindu state, whereas it is secular in the sense of not giving preference to one religion, but respecting all religions. In 1993, the Prime Minister, Shri P.V. Narashima Rao, reaffirmed this secular ideal when he told the Delhi Centennial Day:

> We are not talking of a nation being without any faith or without any religion. . . . We treat all religions exactly alike. . . . We have no first-rate religions and second-rate religions just as we do not have first-rate citizens and second-rate citizens in this country.[12]

Interfaith activity is a challenge to all who have a monolithic view of truth and of society. Those committed to a vision of a society and of a world where people of different faiths live and work harmoniously together have both to reject the heritage of religious prejudice, rivalry and bitterness and to oppose all who would marginalize those of different belief.

It is encouraging that in many religious communities, leaders now recognize the dangers of the "fundamentalist" option and, as we shall see in the next chapter, are not only endorsing the call for interreligious understanding, but arguing for it from the traditional authorities of their religious tradition. This may be the only way in which a religious community can be encouraged to accept new ideas. From traditional sources it is possible to call for people of different faiths to respect each other and perhaps to affirm together certain basic moral values.

Yet the pluralistic interfaith vision rests on radically different presuppositions than those which shaped the traditional thinking of the great religions. The message of tolerance, for example, that Swami Vivekananda proclaimed at the 1893 World's Parliament of Religions, reflected the new emphases of the Hindu renaissance. Today, the possibility is emerging in some quarters of theology becoming an interreligious discipline, or what some have called "ultimology." Also, in what has been called "global spirituality," some people of one faith are absorbing into their spiritual life practices or insights from another faith. These are subjects we shall explore below, including the question of whether eventually a one world religion might emerge.

Leaders and others who endorse interfaith understanding and cooperation from their own traditional sources may find they have embarked upon a journey into uncharted seas.

SIX

Theologies for a Pluralist World

Leaders of major religious communities have in recent years increasingly endorsed the need for inter-religious dialogue. The Archbishop of Canterbury, Dr. George Carey, for example told a Jewish-Christian conference in Jerusalem, "We share in a common task of speaking of the eternal to a world which is dominated by the present." In a world where religious and ethnic pluralism has replaced the dominance of one religion, people of all faiths, he said, should behave towards each other like neighbors. "Dialogue calls us into partnership to work against the domination of one religion to the exclusion of others in any nation state."[1]

Extremism has shocked moderate religious leaders into emphasizing the need for mutual respect. As Dr. Robert Runcie, then Archbishop of Canterbury, said in 1989, "the unexpected shock of the late eighties is to discover that all over the world—in most religions and cultures—there are those who believe they should not tolerate others, should completely avoid those whose beliefs they consider in error."[2]

Following the massacre at Hebron, when a Jewish settler on the West Bank entered the mosque and murdered some thirty Muslims, the Jewish community in Britain was quick to condemn the atrocity. The Chief Rabbi, Dr. Jonathan Sacks, said, "Violence is evil. Violence committed in the name of God is doubly evil. Violence committed against those engaged in worshipping God is unspeakably evil."[3] At the West London Synagogue, a special memorial service for the victims was held; Jeffery Rose, the chairman of the European Board of the World

Union for Progressive Judaism, voiced profound sympathy for the victims of this "totally unacceptable act."[4]

Support for Dialogue from Traditional Sources

In emphasizing the need for mutual respect, religious leaders also stress that this is consistent with deep commitment to a particular faith and the wish to proclaim it. They also have sought to show that mutual respect for those of other religions is taught by the traditional authorities of their religion. This contrasts with the approach of many pioneers of the interfaith movement, such as Unitarians or Baha'is or very liberal members of religions, who spoke of the need for rethinking traditional attitudes. Indeed, in the Christian churches this challenge is still posed by theologians such as John Hick and others who adopt a pluralist position. Yet if a person has first to become a pluralist before seeing the necessity of interreligious understanding, the interfaith movement is likely to remain marginal and be suspected of being an embryonic new religion. The pluralists and universalists, as I shall suggest in a later chapter, remind us that dialogue should be dialogue in truth. It is not just a matter of understanding and respecting what others believe. Dialogue raises questions about our ultimate beliefs.

Even so, it is very important that the major religious communities are persuaded of the need for understanding, mutual respect, and cooperation. This requires argument from traditional sources. A particularly good example is a lecture on "the Interfaith Imperative" by Chief Rabbi, Dr. Jonathan Sacks. In that lecture, he argued strongly from traditional Jewish sources for mutual respect between religions. He pointed out that according to the Rabbis there are thirty-seven occasions in the book of Moses when the command is to love, not the neighbor, but the stranger. Similarly, Jewish mystics used to ask why the stork was an unclean bird. Its name, Chassidah, means the compassionate one. How can a bird called compassion be unclean? But for whom the mystics asked, did the stork have compassion? Only for its own. True compassion knows no bounds. Dr. Sacks also observed that the story of Babel came before the call of Abraham.

> Just as after Babel there is no single universal language, so there is no single universal culture, no single universal tradition and no single universal faith. The faith of Abraham left room for other ways of serving God, just as the English language leaves room for French and Spanish and Italian.[5]

In his Reith Lectures, Dr. Sacks said, "The fact that the great universal monotheisms have not yet formally endorsed a plural world is still the unexorcised darkness at the heart of our religious situation."[6] In "the Interfaith Imperative," he tried to show why this endorsement was true to the Jewish tradition.

Another example of the attempt to find support for dialogue within traditional sources is a paper by Professor Dawud O. S. Noibi on "The Qur'an's Approach to Inter-faith Cooperation." In that paper he made a case for Muslim respect for other faiths on entirely Islamic grounds. In the Qur'an respect is taught for Jews and Christians, who are called "People of the Book." Professor Noibi suggested that this phrase should be translated as "followers of earlier revelations." He stressed that the Qur'an teaches that God has sent every people a prophet, and he suggested that Rama, Krishna, and Zoroaster should be seen as prophets of Allah.[7]

On the same day I listened to Professor Noibi's paper at a conference in New Delhi, I also visited the Jama Masjid in Old Delhi. The guide mentioned that Islam teaches that every people has been sent a prophet, such as Moses or Jesus or Krishna or Rama or Zoroaster. Perhaps the professor from Africa was only acknowledging what Muslims who have lived for centuries in a plural society have long known.

Christian Re-interpretation of Uniqueness

Christians who believe in the uniqueness of Jesus Christ and the universal significance of his saving death have perhaps found it hardest to adjust theologically to a religiously plural world.

Through the centuries the majority attitude has been exclusive, seeing other religions as mistaken or even as the work of the devil. Those who have challenged this view have often been accused of also questioning the uniqueness of Christ. Any Christian exponent of dialogue will have been asked about the verse in St. John's Gospel, "I am the Way, the Truth and the Life. No one cometh to the Father but through me."[8]

Many Christian writers have attempted to combine a more generous view of other faiths with an affirmation of the uniqueness of Christ. I take as an example Cardinal Francis Arinze, who is President of the Pontifical Council for Interreligious Dialogue. He makes clear that "dialogue does not aim at conversion in the sense of a change of religious allegiance." He is well aware that interfaith dialogue is only possible on a basis of mutual respect for the other's view, which conversionist pressure destroys. Yet Cardinal Arinze goes on to affirm that "all human beings are included in the great and unique design of God in Jesus Christ, even when they are not aware of it." That is to say there is one saving act—the death of Christ—for all people, but there are those who benefit from it without conscious faith in Jesus Christ, people who may be called "anonymous Christians."[9]

Professor John Hick and others have shown that this position is unsatisfactory.[10] Yet a pluralist view seems to put you on the margin of the Christian church. At a pragmatic level, if members of the major faith communities are to endorse interreligious cooperation and understanding, they will need to do so in a way that they feel is consistent with traditional claims. Religious communities seldom admit they have been wrong. Rather the tendency is to retranslate, to reinterpret, to add a gloss or to emphasize certain texts and to forget others.

Cardinal Arinze's approach is one attempt to do this, reflecting especially the influence of the Catholic theologian Karl Rahner. I prefer to emphasize the universal significance of Christ rather than his uniqueness. The former stresses the importance of Christ to all people, whereas the latter can be heard by others as devaluing their own religious traditions. As Fr. Gordian Marshall has put it, some Christians are "beginning to recognise a need to work on an understanding of Jesus, which says that the presence of Christians in the world can be a blessing for the whole world without the whole world being Christian."[11] In a similar way, Kenneth Cragg, speaking of Islam, says, "What has authority for some of the human race must have relevance for all. As a 'mercy to the worlds,' Muhammad and the Qur'an cannot well be confined within Islam, nor their significance withheld from those who do not assent to its beliefs.[12]

This reflects a view voiced some time ago by Bishop George Appleton, at one-time Anglican archbishop in Jerusalem.

> Each religion has a mission, a gospel, a central affirmation. Each of us needs to enlarge on the gospel which he has received without wanting to demolish the gospel of others. . . We can enlarge and deepen our initial and basic faith by the experience and insights of people from other religions and cultures, without disloyalty to our own commitment.[13]

Such a position encourages deep commitment to one's own faith, and this is a necessary part of discipleship and worship, without devaluing the faith of others. Each has something valuable to share, and appreciation is more fitting than boasting.

A comparison which helps me is to picture brothers and sisters sitting together after a parent has died. Each will recall his or her own memories. As one listens a fuller picture of the one who had died emerges. Each child had a unique relationship with the parent. If the children have outgrown sibling rivalry, they will treasure each other's memories.

It is also helpful to distinguish the language of worship and that of theology. Worship is the language of a faith community where there are certain shared assumptions. The words are addressed, in the Christian context, to God through Jesus Christ. They have their own logic. It is important that they are in no way triumphalistic nor prejudicial towards others, but they are an expression of a particular commitment. The language of theology, although again the language of a faith community, is the language of logic not of praise. Here there has to be the recognition that if God's love is for people of all faiths, then exclusive terminology is not appropriate. We need to be sensitive to the context of our words and how we use them, to appreciate that theology conveys truth in its own special way.

The Holy Spirit

Another approach adopted by some Christian thinkers is to emphasize the work of the Holy Spirit. This was reflected in the document "Religious Plurality, Theological Perspectives and Affirmations," which was prepared for the Canberra Assembly of the World Council of Churches.[14] This position, particularly favored by members of the Orthodox churches, both maintains the decisive central role of Christ, and the universal work of God's Spirit, active among every people and in every culture. His Beatitude Archbishop Anastasios of Tirana has written in this way of the Holy Spirit.

> 'Present everywhere and filling all things,' in the words of the prayer preceding almost all Orthodox services, the Holy Spirit continues to act for the sanctification of all persons and the fulfilment and completion of the salvation of the whole world: as the Spirit of holiness transferring the breath, love and power of the trinitarian God to human existence and the universe; as the Spirit of power, dynamically renewing the atmosphere in which human beings live and breathe (it is the Holy Spirit who burns up whatever is rotten—concepts, ideas, institutions, customs, demonic structures—and offers new energy for the transforming and renewing of all things in creation); as the Spirit of truth, working and inspiring human beings in their longing and search for truth in any religious setting, every aspect of truth, including scientific, related to human life (this revelation of truth culminates in the decisive knowledge of the mystery of Christ who is the truth par excellence and it is the Spirit who reveals Christ); as the Spirit

of peace calming the hearts and helping to create new relationships among human beings, bringing understanding and reconciliation to the whole of humankind; as the Spirit of justice
giving inspiration and power for people to long and struggle
for peace.[15]

If not only the leaders but also ordinary believers are to feel
at ease with interfaith work, three matters need to be addressed:
the question of mission, the balance of unity and diversity, and
the recognition of peoples' fears.

Mission

Islam and Buddhism as well as Christianity have a sense of
mission, although the questions arise most acutely in the Christian context. They arise in two ways: in the fear of those of
another faith that Christian motivation is suspect and that
dialogue is merely a polite form of mission and, secondly, in the
fear of many Christians that if they do not try to convert others
they are being disloyal to Jesus' command to preach the Gospel
to all nations.

If we believe something to be true or valuable, it is natural to
want to share it. Some years ago, Canon Max Warren noted the
secular usage of "mission" and referred to an article calling on
people to share "the Gospel of Automation." Today many
organizations are writing mission statements. Sharing, which
may be commendable, is easily felt as pressure. This is especially
the case when a person seems concerned for the growth of an
institution. Archbishop Anastasios says that he has always
"experienced difficulty with the word 'mission'" and he is not
the only one. He prefers "martyria," "because it is above all a
personal experience: I saw something, I know something and I
give my witness, my martyria."[16]

I have found that where there is the proper relationship of
trust I can share my deepest convictions and witness to my
experience of God's love in Christ. I will expect the dialogue
partners to share their deepest experiences. All of us, I suspect,

are changed by such sharing in depth: but the motivation is not to convert the other, but to bear witness.

Unity and Diversity

Another difficulty is to give sufficient weight both to the diversity of religious belief and practice and yet to point to the unity. A particular feature of *Sarva-Dharma-Sammelana* at Bangalore was the recognition that differences are enriching rather than a threat. The unity was discovered not at the level of intellectual agreement but of friendship and trust, where the other was valued as other. This was especially notable at the times of prayer. Members of one faith offered their prayers as a gift which they hoped their guests would share.

At some meetings I tried to make the point by referring to food. Many peoples' diet today is enriched by food from around the world. Indeed interfaith gatherings sometimes have delicious international meals. At a beach cafe in India I was interested to see a big advertisement for English porridge. Yet, while enjoying new dishes, most people tend to base their diet on dishes that they are used to.

Differences as well as unity are, I believe, God-given. The special witness of each religious tradition relates to its particularity. In our international world, there has also been a growth of nationalism, for example among the Welsh or the Basques. Perhaps many of us can only feel at ease if we are secure in our particular identity.

What Are We Afraid Of ?

If more believers are to be involved in interfaith activity, they may have to be helped to see that it need not be a threat to their faith identity. Indeed, as so many have discovered, interfaith dialogue may well lead to a deepening, as well as a broadening of one's faith.

This is not the only fear. Not long ago, a Christian woman telephoned me and asked, "I want to meet some people of another faith. How do I set about it?" It reminded me of how common is the fear of the unfamiliar. How long will I have to sit cross-legged on the floor? Will I be given unfamiliar food? If I am going to be asked to take my shoes off, are there holes in my socks? One report on multi-faith worship warns that "places of worship of all faiths are often ill-equipped with toilets."[17] Will I be expected to bow to an idol or eat *prasad*—a sweet food given to worshippers?

Fear of the unfamiliar is common. This is why so much of the work of interfaith organizations has been devoted to encouraging people to meet. Dr. Pauline Webb has said, "The pot of tea shared in a multi-racial fellowship meeting may seem a small enough gesture, but it can be a foretaste of the Kingdom of God."[18] The regular visits to one another's places of worship, arranged by local interfaith groups, are a vital means of overcoming fears and misunderstanding.

There are also fears of what is hidden, for instance, of exposing memories of past prejudice. Some Jews feel uncomfortable, if they visit a church, at looking at a crucifix. There are fears too that the dialogue may have a hidden political agenda. For example, some have felt that Christian-Jewish dialogue was used to win friends for Israel, while some Christian-Muslim dialogue has been used to attack Zionism. Again, Christian dialogue with exponents of classical Hinduism has been felt by the Dalits to ignore present day social oppression. Others fear that by meeting with new religious movements they give respectability to such bodies. Among some minority groups there is the fear that interfaith cooperation will absorb them into the majority culture and threaten their identity.[19]

There is a fear too among some people that dialogue presupposes the values of the Enlightenment. In a review of the life of a Christian-Jewish dialogue group of which I was a member for some years, Rabbi Dr. Norman Solomon began by noting that our discourse was in English.

Three cultures—even three civilizations—met. A Christian

civilization, a Jewish civilization, and the third civilization, in which all of us Jews and Christians live and find our identity, and which was mediated through the English language. This third was the civilization of modernity or of enlightenment.[20]

Similarly, Dr. Stanley Samartha has drawn attention to the fact that most dialogue takes place in English and that often the initiatives and the assumptions have been Christian, as indeed they were at the World's Parliament of Religions in Chicago in 1893.[21] This is one reason also why interfaith organizations need to broaden the composition of their leadership, which is still too Western. Recently, however, I have noticed that members of many different faith communities are taking initiatives in arranging interfaith events.

While extremists in religious communities are not interested in dialogue, it is important to extend dialogue as widely as possible. Interfaith dialogue needs to be broadly based if people of different religions are to live together in peace. It requires genuine openness to a wide range of beliefs, and those who promote dialogue need to be sensitive to peoples' fears and to be very aware of the dangers of imposing their agenda or their assumptions. The endorsement of interfaith activity by a growing number of designated religious leaders and the sympathetic interest of some political leaders is welcome.[22] More popular support is still needed, especially if the aspirations of the interfaith movement are to be effective in changing the world.

SEVEN

The Declaration Towards A Global Ethic

The declaration of a Global Ethic was intended to be the crowning achievement of the Chicago Parliament of the World's Religions in August 1993. In fact, however, its impact was somewhat muted by disagreements. Even so, it represents a significant step forward in the search for a consensus on moral values, which many people believe is a necessary requirement for a peaceful world and for stable national societies.

Such a Declaration would have delighted Charles Bonney, whose idea it was to hold the 1893 Parliament. One of his objectives for the Parliament was "to unite all Religion against all irreligion; to make the Golden Rule the basis of this union; and to present to the world. . . the substantial unity of many religions in the good deeds of the religious life."[1] In his opening address to the Parliament, Bonney hoped that the Congress would demonstrate to the world the brotherhood of religions.[2] Again, in his closing address he affirmed "Henceforth the religions of the world will make war, not on each other, but on the giant evils that afflict mankind."[3] At the Parliament there was considerable discussion of moral and social matters.

The hope that members of different religions, while disagreeing on matters of belief, might agree on moral values has remained a conviction of those active in various interfaith organizations. Several attempts have been made to voice a shared view on moral and social issues.[4]

The Preparation of a Declaration
Towards A Global Ethic

The need for such a moral consensus was the central argument of Hans Küng's *Global Responsibility*. Now that modern communications have made the world one society, it needs, he said, an agreed ethic. Despite their differences of belief, people of faith should articulate the basic moral values which they hold in common. He concluded the book with these words:

> No human life without a world ethic for the nations. No peace among the nations without peace among the religions. No peace among the religions without dialogue among the religions.[5]

Even before this book was published, discussions had begun between Hans Küng and the (Chicago) Council for a Parliament of the World's Religions about the possibility of preparing a Declaration of a Global Ethic in time for the Parliament. There was, however, some delay in pursuing this. Meanwhile Professor Leonard Swidler of Temple University, Philadelphia, who is the Editor of the *Journal of Ecumenical Studies*, wrote an appeal which included a call for the composition of a declaration on a global ethos.

> Efforts should concentrate on drawing together the research and reflection on Global Ethic and related matters into a "Universal Declaration on a Global Ethos," which would then be circulated to the various forums of all the religions and ethical groups for appropriate revisions—with a view to eventual adoption by all the religions and ethical groups of the world. Such a "Universal Declaration of a World Ethos" could then serve a function similar to the 1948 "Universal Declaration of Human Rights" of the United Nations—a kind of standard that all will be expected to live up to. . . The "Universal Declaration of the Global Ethos" would in a major way bring to bear the moral and spiritual resources of all the religions and ethical groups on the basic ethical problems of the world, which are not easily susceptible to political force.[6]

The appeal was signed by a number of important theologians of different religions and by some scholars in religious studies. It was not until early 1992 that the Chicago preparatory

Council formally asked Hans Küng to undertake the draft of a Declaration of a Global Ethic. Already there was some difference between the Council's expectation of a short statement and Hans Küng's view that a longer document was necessary. The time for adequate consultation was also very limited. Nonetheless, Küng accepted the invitation and devoted his teaching program for the summer semester to an inter-disciplinary and inter-religious colloquium on "Human Rights—World Religions—World Ethic." Distinguished members of the world's religions participated in this colloquium and helped to shape Küng's thinking. Küng also consulted widely and, during the summer and autumn of 1992, circulated a number of drafts to a group of scholars.

On October 23rd, Küng was in a position to send a draft, translated into English by Professor Leonard Swidler, to Chicago. His hope was to have their corrections by the end of the year so that a definitive text could then be prepared. Küng's text was shown to all the Trustees of the Chicago Parliament and to a number of experts and religious leaders. However, it was not until June 1993, when Küng was preoccupied with another seminar on a different topic, that he received an answer to the draft which he had sent in October 1992. The reply was positive, only asking for some improvements to the translation and some corrections to content and style. The short summary, produced by a Chicago committee, was also attached. Küng now incorporated most of the suggestions and sent to Chicago the definitive English text, again translated by Professor Swidler, on July 17th, 1993—only a little more than a month before the opening of the Parliament.

It had been hoped to present the *Declaration* to some internationally known representatives of the great religions for examination and acceptance prior to the Chicago Parliament, but time did not allow for this. The text was sent to those invited to be Presidents of the Parliament and to the members of the Assembly of Religious and Spiritual Leaders, which was to meet during the Parliament, but not to other participants.

There was to be a press embargo on the text until September 4, the final day of the Parliament, but this was quickly broken.

The intention was that the three hundred individual members of the Assembly should be invited, in a personal capacity, to endorse and sign the Declaration. Much of the time at the Assembly was spent in small groups. Opportunity was provided for the discussion of the Global Ethic, but there was no chance to make changes to the text. The procedure at the Assembly was not made clear to participants and there was some resentment. In the end it was agreed to rename the document as *Towards a Global Ethic: An Initial Declaration*. The hope is that it will be the basis of widespread discussion and improvement. At the closing open-air ceremony of the Parliament, the Introduction was read and applauded by the large crowd.

There are several questions about the procedure. Were enough people consulted? Küng says that "more than a hundred people from all the great religions had been involved in the process of consultation" (GE.52). Would it have been better if the initiative had been taken not just by the Chicago Council alone but in consultation with international interfaith organizations? Is there now an adequate mechanism for further consultation? Does the Introduction, which in effect is now called "The Declaration" by the Chicago Council, do justice to the full text?

To better understand the significance of the full document, it will be helpful to consider first the Principles prepared by Hans Küng, then to look at the Introduction, and finally to consider the various criticisms made of the *Declaration*, which, in this discussion, refers to the entire document.

The Principles of the Global Ethic

The text prepared by Hans Küng begins with the assumptions on which it is based. Our world, it is claimed, is experiencing a fundamental crisis in global economy, global ecology and global politics, together with the lack of "a grand vision" (GE 17). Too often religion is used to incite aggression and fanaticism. The world can only move away from its present crisis by adopting a global ethic, which can already be found within the religious teachings of the world. By a global ethic is meant "a minimal fundamental consensus concerning binding values, irrevocable standards and fundamental moral attitudes" (GE18).

Two principles are then affirmed. First that there will be "no new global order without a new global ethic," and that "every human being must be treated humanely" (GE 18-24). These are based on arguments which Küng had already outlined in his *Global Responsibility*. The first section of that book, as we have seen,[7] talks of a paradigm shift from modernity to post-modernity. One aspect of this is that we now live in a global society but have not yet found a way of living together.

It is as a contribution to this that the Global Ethic is offered. It is no longer appropriate in a democratic society for the state to determine moral values, nor can they be imposed by one religious community (GR 27). Yet no society exists if there are not some basic shared values. Different groups may live in geographical proximity, but without shared values there is no society.

> If the different world-views within a society are to live together, the pluralistic society in particular needs a basic consensus to which these world-views contribute, to bring about the formation of a consensus which is not 'strict,' but 'overlapping.' (GR 27-8)

If the consensus is not to be based on the moral teaching of one particular faith, what is the criterion to be? Küng's answer is the *humanum*. "The basic ethical question in terms of criteria is: What is good for human beings? The answer is: What helps them to be what is not at all obvious, i.e. truly human" (GR 90). That which is good is that which helps people to be authentically human, to develop their full potential. Küng argues that the purpose of each religion is to encourage such authentic humanity. The paths to salvation may differ, but religious traditions agree in rejecting murder, lying, theft, sexual exploitation and encouraging respect for parents and children. The golden rule can be found in each tradition (GR 58). Küng accepts various recent "self-potential" movements, provided they are not detached from responsibility for others (GR 31).

The *Declaration* recognizes the great differences within and between religious traditions on ethical matters, but affirms that there is also enough agreement for this to be publicly proclaimed (GE 22). "In the face of all humanity our religious and ethical convictions demand that every human being must be treated humanely" (GE 23). This means that every person without any distinction has an "inalienable and untouchable dignity" and "every human is obliged to behave in a genuinely human fashion, to do good and avoid evil" (GE 23). The *Declaration* then seeks to clarify what this means, namely, the "irrevocable, unconditional ethical norms" (GE 23).

Four Irrevocable Directives

The *Declaration* identifies these as four irrevocable directives found in most of the religions of the world.

These four broad, ancient guidelines are:

1. Commitment to a culture of non-violence and respect for life.

2. Commitment to a culture of solidarity and a just economic order.

3. Commitment to a culture of tolerance and a life of truthfulness.

4. Commitment to a culture of equal rights and partnership between men and women.

The implications of each commitment are outlined below.

*Commitment to a culture of non-violence
and respect for life*

A commitment to non-violence means that

no one has the right physically or psychically to torture, injure, much less kill, any other human being. And no people, no state, no race, no religion has the right to hate, to discriminate against, to "cleanse," to exile, much less to liquidate a "foreign" minority which is different in behaviour or holds different beliefs (GE 25).

Conflicts should be resolved without violence within a framework of justice. Those in political power should seek the most non-violent and peaceful solutions possible. The *Declaration*, as Küng points out in response to criticism by some Muslims, does not adopt a pacifist position but pleads for the minimum of violence. It warns that armament is a mistaken path.

Children need to be brought up in a culture of non-violence in home and school. The lives of animals and plants also deserve protection for "we are all intertwined together in this cosmos" (GE 26).

The spirit of non-violence is not just negative, it implies an active concern for the welfare of others. Individuals and groups should show respect, indeed high appreciation, for every other person and all should protect and support all minorities.

*Commitment to a culture of solidarity
and a just economic order*

The second commitment implies criticism of economic exploitation, unbridled capitalism, greed, and corruption. The command not to steal means that no one has the right to dispossess others nor to neglect the needs of society and the Earth. Extremes of poverty make violence likely so that there will be no global peace without global economic justice. Young people need to learn that property and possessions carry obligations. The plight of the poorest billions requires a more just world economy and particularly a resolution of the world debt crisis. To be authentically human, it is said, means using political power for service to humanity and there should be "a spirit of compassion with those who suffer, with special care for the children, the aged, the poor, the disabled, the refugees, and the lonely" (GE 29). Moderation and modesty are to be cultivated instead of greed, competition and excessive display of wealth.

*Commitment to a culture of tolerance
and a life of truthfulness*

The third commitment to tolerance and truthfulness is especially challenging to politicians, those who work in the mass media, to scientists, and to "representatives of religions who dismiss other religions as of little value and who preach fanaticism and intolerance instead of respect and understanding" (GE 30). The need of young people to learn truthfulness at home and school is affirmed. Allowing in a plural society for the variety of opinions should not mean indifference to truth.

*Commitment to a culture of equal rights and partnership
between men and women*

The fourth commitment calls for equal rights and partnership between men and women. Sexual exploitation and discrimination is condemned. Young people need to learn at home and in school that "sexuality is not a negative, destructive, or exploitative force, but creative and affirmative" (GE 33). Sexuality should express and reinforce a loving relationship lived by equal partners. Marriage, despite all its cultural and religious variety, is characterized by love, loyalty, and permanence. All exploitation, including exploitation of children, is to be rejected.

Transformation of Consciousness

The final section of the *Declaration* speaks of the need for a transformation in the consciousness of individuals and in public life. Already such a transformation is being glimpsed in such areas as war and peace, the economy, and ecology. Now there must be a transformation of ethics and values. The difficulty of reaching a consensus on many disputed questions is acknowledged, but it is said that in many professions there is a new awareness of ethical responsibility. Religious communities are encouraged to formulate their own very specific ethic. This is important as the intention of *Toward a Global Ethic* is not to reduce moral concern to a lowest common denominator but to identify what is already agreed between the different teachings of the great faiths and to use this as a basis for building a greater consensus.

The *Declaration* recognizes the need for the conversion of the heart which is possible through the awakening of our spiritual powers through reflection, meditation, prayer, or positive thinking. It ends with an appeal that the consciousness of individuals needs to be changed and with a commitment of those who sign it "to a global ethic, to better mutual understanding, as well as to socially-beneficial, peace-fostering and Earth-friendly ways of Life" (GE 36). The concluding words are "We invite all men and women, whether religious or not, to do the same" (GE 36). Unlike some documents coming from conferences, which end with resolutions criticizing others and telling them what to do, this *Declaration* is an expression of commitment by those who sign it.

Küng's Commentary

In his commentary on the *Declaration* in his book, *A Global Ethic*, Küng explains what he felt it should and should not be. The ethical level had to be distinguished from the legal and political. The *Declaration* had to avoid duplicating the UN Declaration on Human Rights, not least because an ethic is more than rights. The *Declaration* had also to avoid being a political manifesto and a moral sermon. As a document of consensus, it also had to avoid disputed matters such as divorce or euthanasia. The *Declaration* also could not be a philosophical treatise nor be "an enthusiastic religious proclamation." The aim was to penetrate to a deeper ethical level, identifying "binding values, irrevocable criteria and inner basic attitudes" (GE 58). The *Declaration* needed to be capable of securing a consensus, related to reality, and generally comprehensible. It also had to show that religions can be self-critical.

The *Declaration*, Küng says, also needed a religious foundation, even though it was also addressed to people who were not religious. This may make it surprising that there is no reference in the document to God. Some might even have expected it to be promulgated as if in the name of God, echoing the Biblical phrase "Thus saith the Lord." The use of the word "God," however, created difficulties for Buddhists and might have alienated those who are non-religious. Küng in his commentary explains the Buddhist difficulty with the word "God" and notes that at the Assembly there was a protest from some Buddhists that many of the invocations at the Parliament were addressed to God (GE 64).

The Introduction

If the search for agreement to the *Declaration* was not entirely well-served by the procedure at the Parliament's Assembly of Religious and Spiritual Leaders, it may also be that the Intro-duction prepared by a Chicago committee was also in some ways unhelpful. It will certainly be a pity if that comes to be taken as the *Declaration*, instead of the full document. (In fact, Parliament publications do name what I'm calling the Introduc-tion as the "Declaration of a Global Ethic," while Küng's work is titled "The Principles of a Global Ethic.") However, the Introduction does not explain the context or rationale of the *Declaration* and in some places, for example, in affirming non-violence or condemning sexual immorality, it eliminates the nuances of the full text. Like the Principles, it begins with the world's agony, but loses the need for vision.

Criticisms

At the Assembly of Religious and Spiritual Leaders

In addition to criticism of the procedure at the Parliament's Assembly, there were also some criticisms of the content. These were voiced at the round table discussions, but not all were expressed to the whole meeting. Some Muslims, particularly aware of the situation in Bosnia, were concerned that the section on non-violence denied a people's right to self defense. This may appear to be true of the Introduction, but not of the full text, as Küng points out (GE 68). It was said that the

Declaration says too little about the family. The emphasis on equal rights for men and women troubled some members of the Assembly. A third objection was that the document was "too Western," but as Küng says, any document will in part reflect the approach and style of the person who drafts it.

Despite the criticisms, Küng notes that no one questioned the central core of the Declaration.

> No side put in question the need for a *Declaration Toward a Global Ethic* and its usefulness. The basic ethical requirement that "Every human being must be treated humanely" was accepted as a matter of course. . . and the second complementary basic demand, the Golden Rule, was similarly accepted as a matter of course. (GE 71)

At Bangalore

The lack of a sense of vision was a major criticism of the document made at *Sarva-Dharma-Sammelana* at Bangalore. It had been hoped that the comments of the group at Bangalore which studied an advance copy of the document might be reflected in the final declaration, but in fact there was not time to alter the Chicago text even if there had been a desire to do so. The Bangalore comments and their revision of the Introduction are interesting and may contribute to a future revision of the *Declaration*.[8]

The Bangalore workshop was attended by between thirty and forty people. Members' attention was also drawn to the Mt. Abu Declaration which emerged from the "Global Cooperation for a Better World" Programme.[9] This document reflects "The Peoples' Vision of a Better World." It may be that this document influenced members of the Bangalore group in their suggestion that "the sequence of agony before all else seems mistaken: pain and confession are necessary before the full affirmation of ethical concerns, but we prefer a positive opening passage."[10] The Bangalore revision therefore begins,

> Our world is precious, fragile, and beautiful. The earth and

her people need to be cherished and nurtured with care and vision. They can survive and flourish only if a shared world ethic is both affirmed and followed.[11]

The Bangalore group questioned the title "Declaration," saying that it purports to be inclusive and invitational to all. Yet as the first signatories are religious leaders it may appear pretentious or presumptuous. The group suggested it should be renamed as an "Affirmation" or "Contribution." In similar mood, the group felt that the language should be directional rather than directive and that imperatives should be replaced by commitments and invitations. "This is more than a question of style or language but of whether religions are seen as essentially passing judgement or energizing ethical response."[12]

The Bangalore group also suggested that the Introduction should contain more specific references to the plight of children and of the unemployed. There was also some unease about the sentence on sexuality.

A more serious criticism of the whole project was made by Professor Fr. John B. Chethimattam, of Dharmaram College, Bangalore, who was previously a Professor at Fordham University. He questioned the possibility of separating the moral concepts of a religion from its total vision. Each religion has its particular moral teaching which is related holistically to its faith and life. He strongly objected to the universalizing implied by the project. "The very label of 'a Global Ethic' smacks of an imperialist plot to continue its domination on the majority of humanity through specious moral preaching." Professor Chethimattam suggested that besides the evils listed more attention should have been paid to the fact that the great majority of humanity, especially women and the low caste and marginalized people, have no say in the direction of their lives. Attention should also have been drawn to the racism and casteism that are rampant. He mentions also the evil of widespread corruption and the great profit made by the sale of weapons of destruction to the poorest nations. Professor Chethimattam also challenges the religions to show far greater repentance for the "atrocities perpetrated in the past in the name of religion."[13]

Others have also questioned whether an ethic is independent of the religious tradition of which it is part. This, I think, mistakes Küng's intention which is not to replace particular ethical teaching but to indicate to the world, in which many people are skeptical about or disinterested in religion, that despite the appearance of rivalry, religions do agree on certain basic ethical values. This is also why religious communities have a contribution to make to global issues which have a spiritual and moral dimension.

KCRP

In South Korea, at a meeting arranged by the Korean Conference on Religion and Peace in Seoul, held two months after the Chicago Parliament, there was further discussion of the *Declaration*. This prompted a member of the meeting to submit a Korean version of the *Declaration*, which was received with applause. The main point here was a wish to move away from the focus on the *humanum* and to stress the unity of all life. It was felt that the *Declaration* is too anthropocentric.

> We have come to believe that the earth, heaven, all that lives on earth and all humanity comprise one life-community organically interdependent. Thus, we judge that all kinds of oppression, exploitation and domination are unjust destruction of this life-community.[14]

The document also contains a special mention of the situation in Korea, where North and South are still divided. In the discussion, it was said that in Asia there has never been the enmity between religions that has existed in Europe. This, it was said, relates to a different understanding of Truth. This is probably true of East Asia, although recent troubles in India and Sri Lanka hardly suggest it is true of that subcontinent.

A similar concern—that the *Declaration* is too anthropocentric —has been voiced by Paul Waldau in a paper called "Beyond Praise of the Declaration of World Religions." He complains that the document threatens to perpetuate the traditional view that "of all the species on this earth, the only one which is of significance as a species, and therefore as individuals, is the human species."[15]

What Use Is a Declaration of a Global Ethic?

The question remains: will the Declaration do any good? Hans Küng addresses this in his Preface.

> The hope is that this document may set off a process which changes the behaviour of men and women in the religions in the direction of understanding, respect and cooperation. And if all goes well, in the not too distant future, we shall have other declarations which make the global ethic of the religions more precise and concrete and add further illustrations to it. But is not such an expectation sheer illusion? Can the religions be expected to accept such a declaration? Are such hopes realistic? To the eternal sceptics and pessimists we would say: No one will deny that within the space of two or three decades it has proved possible to bring about worldwide a universal change of awareness about economics and ecology, about world peace and disarmament, and about the partnership between men and women. Our document here has been written and approved in the hope that a similar change of awareness may take place over a basic ethic common to all humankind, a global ethic. It is up to the religions of this earth and to all peoples all over the world, in a quite practical way, wherever they are, to make sure that this declaration remains more than paper, that it is filled with life, that it inspires people to a life of mutual respect, understanding and cooperation.[16]

If the intention of the *Declaration* is to stimulate awareness and transformation, then attention needs to be given to the educational uses of the document.

Education

There is concern in many countries that young people do not identify with the traditional moral values of their community. They may reject the religious beliefs with which those moral traditions are associated and in so doing reject the moral teaching and values as well.

Toward a Global Ethic does not require *a priori* membership of a faith community nor acceptance of particular religious beliefs. It starts with the question "What is good for human beings? What helps them to be truly human?" (GR 90). This is an open question on which one may expect most people and most young people to have opinions. What do they think makes for their own fulfillment and how does this relate to the aspirations of others? When a group have agreed on their answers to the questions they could compare these with answers given by other people and the answers given by the great religious traditions. In a society where many people do not have a religious faith, moral teaching cannot be based on a particular authority. It needs to be autonomous. Yet it can be seen that essential moral insights are shared by all the great faiths.

The discussion of which moral insights are held in common and which are distinctive would be a helpful way to quicken young people's moral discernment and awareness of different faith traditions. The *Declaration* could well form the basis for a useful values or character education project, appropriately designed for young people.[17] It may well be that it is through its educational applications that the *Declaration* will have its greatest impact.

A Continuing Discussion

The *Declaration Toward a Global Ethic* continues to be a subject of debate and discussion. A number of conferences have focused upon it, a few books have reproduced it, and articles have appeared on the subject. It is not clear whether those who promoted this project hope that eventually a revised, more widely accepted *Declaration* will emerge, or whether the *Declaration* has achieved its purpose by stimulating discussion and reflection. If, as Dr. Swidler hoped, a Universal Declaration of a Global Ethos could serve a similar function to the United Nations' Universal Declaration on Human Rights, then revision and wider agreement is necessary.

Questions about the *Declaration* point to others such as how to build upon past development of the interfaith movement as well as on the significant events of 1993. These topics along with a survey of activities up to Fall of 1997 and some future plans are discussed in the next chapter.

EIGHT

New Developments and a New Agenda

Since 1993 there has been rapid growth of interfaith activity throughout the world, with increasing emphasis on its practical importance.

The number of local interfaith groups has increased in several countries. National bodies such as the North American Interfaith Network, the Inter Faith Network for the United Kingdom, and the Interreligious Coordinating Council of Israel have become established and have a record of solid achievement. National bodies for interfaith work are also being set up in several other countries, such as Mozambique or Jordan. Just as the established international organizations have increasingly focused on practical projects, the same is true of recently-established international interfaith organizations.

Developments Since 1993 in Established Organizations

Since 1993, both the World Conference on Religion and Peace and the International Association for Religious Freedom have held major international conferences.

World Conference on Religion and Peace (WCRP)

Nearly 1000 people from 63 countries attended WCRP's Sixth World Assembly, which was held in Vatican City and Riva del Garda, Italy, in November 1994. The theme was "Healing the World: Religions for Peace." In an opening address, Pope John Paul II stressed the fact that "religion and peace go together" and added that "to wage war in the name of religion is a blatant contradiction." Participants discussed many urgent problems such as respect for human rights, the protection of children, and the restoration of ecological harmony.

Concern for reducing violence and war and for building peace and security remain a priority for WCRP. Its members are actively engaged in efforts at reconciliation and peace building in several parts of the world, especially in Sarajevo, which was devastated by the hostilities in former Yugoslavia. A concern for economic justice was uppermost at WCRP's European Conference held at Dobogoko, near Budapest in Hungary in October 1996.

International Association for Religious Freedom (IARF)

IARF held its 29th Congress at Won Kwang University in Iksan (Iri) City, South Korea, in August 1996. The theme was Spirituality–Responsibility–Cooperation. Study groups discussed economic justice, religious practice, religion and culture, religious education, and ecological living. A significant aspect of the Congress was the increased understanding and reconciliation it created between Korean and Japanese member groups.

The number of IARF member groups continues to grow and the regional structure of the organization has been strengthened. IARF has been active in resisting all that threatens freedom of religion and belief and in expressing its solidarity with minority religious groups. The next Assembly is planned for Vancouver in 1999.

World Congress of Faiths (WCF)

In 1996, the WCF marked its sixtieth anniversary with several events: a tour to Tibet to identify with the suffering of the Tibetans; a significant lecture by the Archbishop of Canterbury, Dr. George Carey, on "How far Can We Travel Together?" and the publication of my history of WCF, *A Wider Vision*.[2] WCF, in publicizing the *Declaration Toward a Global Ethic*, has been working to see how it could be used in the character or values education of young people. A resource book on multifaith prayer, *All in Good Faith*, was published in 1997.

WCF has also been seeking to help health workers, police, and others with community responsibilities to appreciate the challenges and opportunities of living in a religiously plural society.

Temple of Understanding

In 1997 the Temple of Understanding merged its work with the newly-established Interfaith Center of New York, which has been set up by Very Rev. James Parks Morton, formerly Dean of the Episcopal Cathedral of St. John the Divine and President of the Temple of Understanding. The Center has three main areas of work: first, a long term education program with a particular emphasis on children and youth; secondly, an international program in close coordination with the United Nations and its specialized agencies; and, thirdly, a program of spiritual artistic and cultural events intended to increase the wider public's appreciation of the world's faith traditions. Although the Center is primarily for New Yorkers, because New York is an international city and because the UN's headquarters are there, the Center is bound also to have an international dimension to its work, thus enhancing the Temple of Understanding's outreach.

New Developments in New Organizations

Council for a Parliament of the World's Religions (CPWR)

At the conclusion of the 1893 World's Parliament of Religions there was talk of a continuing program, but nothing materialized. For a moment it seemed possible that the same might happen in 1993. Very quickly, however, the CPWR found the energy to launch both the Metropolitan Interreligious Initiative in the Chicago area and the International Interreligious Initiative. Chicago is perhaps the most cosmopolitan city in the world and CPWR's Metropolitan Initiative is actively encouraging grassroots dialogue and cooperation there.

The International Initiative, under the leadership of Jim Kenney, has a threefold focus for its work: holding future

Parliaments of the world's religions, promoting discussion of the 1993 *Declaration Towards A Global Ethic*, and, thirdly, Projects 2000. The CPWR seeks to facilitate new parliaments to be held every five years in different parts of the world. Plans are now well advanced for a Parliament in South Africa in late 1999.

A new, preparatory Assembly of Religious and Spiritual Leaders—the first such assembly met during the 1993 Parliament—was convened in November 1997. This Assembly offered advice in preparation for the 1999 Parliament of the World's Religions in Capetown and helped with the agenda for the next Parliament's Assembly of Religious and Spiritual Leaders. The '97 Assembly also helped in drafting a "Call to Our Guiding Institutions," which is intended to open up dialogue between the religions and the institutions of government, business, education, and the media, which do so much to shape national and international life.

CPWR also intends to publicize the *Global Ethic* in new ways and to work with other organizations that are engaged in promoting understanding of the ethical common ground of the world's religions. Through Projects 2000 in cooperation with the Millennium Institute of Washington, DC, CPWR is encouraging all religious communities, as well as nations and other groups, to use the millennial moment to offer "millennial threshold gifts" that will make a long-term difference to the planetary community.

The Peace Council

Another development from the Parliament that is not a part of CPWR is the Peace Council, which is the brain-child of Dr. Daniel Gómez Ibáñez, who was Executive Director of the Parliament and is now Executive Director of the Peace Council. The Peace Council, which met for the first time at Windsor Castle, near London, in November 1995, brings together a small but diverse group of religious and spiritual individuals who are internationally known and respected. By working together they hope to strengthen their efforts for peace.

The authority and influence of the Peace Council depends upon the moral authority of its members. Members of the Peace Council include Dr. Oscar Arias Sanchez, former President of Costa Rica and 1987 Nobel Peace laureate; Dr. Dalil Boubaker, Rector of the Islamic Institute at the Paris Mosque; Samdech Preah Maha Ghosananda, supreme leader of Cambodian Buddhism; H. H. the Dalai Lama; Archbishop Desmond Tutu, and several other remarkable spiritual leaders.

The programs of the Council are intended to help people and communities grow in the ways of peace. The Peace Council has become active in the campaign to ban land mines and has arranged interfaith prayer services at major conferences on this issue that were held in Brussels, Geneva, and Mozambique. Some Councilors also took part in a three-week peace walk in Cambodia led by Samdech Preah Maha Ghosananda.

The second meeting of the Council was held in San Cristóbal de las Casas, in Chiapas, Mexico, to support the work of Bishop Samuel Ruiz Garcia, a Peace Councilor who is active in efforts at mediation and in defense of human rights. The Council has also assisted the establishment of a Home of Peace and Love near Bangkok, which provides shelter and help to pregnant victims of prostitution and rape.

United Religions Initiative (URI)

Another major development, the United Religions Initiative, owes its genesis to the Fiftieth Anniversary of the signing of the United Nations Charter at San Francisco in June 1995. Commemorative events included an interfaith service for UN leaders and the religious community at Grace Cathedral and an interfaith conference of young people from many countries at the University of San Francisco. In thinking about the service, Bishop Swing, the Episcopal bishop of California, had the dream of "a place where the world's faith communities, continuing to respect each other's distinctiveness, could meet together on a daily and permanent basis in a place of their own."[3] For fifty years the nations of the world had sought to be in dialogue and act together for the common good. Was it not time, Bishop Bill Swing asked himself, for religions to do the same?

Following the 1995 conference, Bishop Swing traveled around the world, meeting with many religious leaders and those active in interfaith work. In June 1996, some 55 leaders from several religions and countries met in San Francisco to create a plan to move towards the writing of a charter. In 1997, regional conferences were held in Oxford, New York, and Buenos Aires and an international gathering was held in June at Stanford University, near San Francisco. Additional regional conferences are being arranged throughout the world by staff and by the Rev. Charles Gibbs, URI's Executive Director.

The June 1997 gathering, with 200 participants, was full of enthusiasm. From it emerged some twenty task forces to explore aspects of URI's development. The range of ideas was a little bewildering and it is not clear, at the time of writing, how URI will develop and be structured. As someone at the conference said, with tongue-in-cheek, "We don't need to do a feasibility study because this UR vision is unfeasible."

It is important to clarify that the United Religions Initiative is a *process* working towards the creation of a United Religions organization. If it is to achieve its initial high purpose—one that more than a few visionary souls have dreamed of during this century—it needs to be owned by the religions themselves rather than by interfaith enthusiasts. The last fifty years have seen a growing number of religious leaders identify with interfaith work. Some organizations, especially WCRP, have gotten high level backing, but mostly the energy for interfaith work has come from individuals rather than from official religious authorities. Religious communities remain reluctant to fund the work.

The moment may now have come for this breakthrough; certainly the world community, especially the United Nations, is more aware that religion has a vital role to play in the search for world peace. Yet URI in some ways seems to be more of a grassroots development and at this stage much of the energy comes from spiritual movements and highly-motivated individuals rather than from organized religions. Perhaps URI will create such a popular ground-swell that religious bodies will be encouraged to endorse it and back the creation of a United Religions.

Other Initiatives

A few other important initiatives that we can note only briefly include: Interfaith International, whose President is His Eminence Sayyed Muhammed Musawi; the World Fellowship of Interreligious Councils, which marked its twenty-fifth anniversary with an international conference in Cochin, India, in 1996; and the Center for World Thanksgiving, of Dallas, Texas, whose mission is to promote the giving of thanks as a healing and uniting activity for people of all faiths.

I would not want to give the impression that, because I have concentrated above on new initiatives based in the USA, interfaith activity is just a Western concern. Some Japanese religious groups, especially Rissho Kosei-kei, have a long record of distinguished work in this field, and the Won Buddhists of Korea have taken important initiatives.

Indeed one reason for encouragement is that interfaith activity is now a genuinely international and interreligious endeavor. Groups both new and established in all parts of the world are actively engaged in the search for inter-religious dialogue and cooperation, and more and more religious leaders are endorsing this work.

A New Agenda

In the four years since the 1993 Parliament of the World's Religions, as I hope I have shown, there has been considerable growth of interfaith activity. There has also been an increasing emphasis on its practical importance. Indeed, I see 1993 as a milestone in the growth of the interfaith movement. The focus has changed from trying to get people of different religions together to discovering what people of faith can do together for our world. Paul Knitter, for example, argues in his recent *One Earth, Many Religions* that "concern for the widespread suffering that grips humanity and threatens the planet can and must be the 'common cause' for all religions."[4] Hans Küng, in his *A Global Ethic for Global Politics and Economics,* seeks to show how moral principles can and should be applied to the affairs of the world.[5] For myself, during the Year of Inter-religious Understanding and Cooperation in 1993, I came to see that we were not just talking about cooperation between religious people, but about cooperation within national societies and between nations as essential for our life together.

Despite the very practical efforts of some groups, up until 1993 much of the energy in the interfaith movement had to go into persuading people of different faiths to meet. There was first of all ignorance and quite often hostility to overcome. People of one faith knew little about another faith and what they knew was often erroneous. A second task was encouraging people of different faiths to get to know each other, to relax in each other's company, to talk and perhaps to become friends. As prejudices were dispelled and friendship grew, many people found they had to rethink their attitudes toward the members and theologies of other religions.

Now, however, many people long for the religions to be "the moral conscience of humanity," as Pope John Paul II expressed it to the Assisi World Day of Prayer for Peace. This new agenda reflects the fact that the great problems that threaten human life and the environment concern us all, just because of our common humanity. Since 1993, as we have seen, several international interfaith bodies have focused on practical questions.

The question now is what effect does all this work have. Indeed, the subject of two of the conferences of the International Interfaith Centre at Oxford—to be described more fully below—have been "How effective is interfaith activity in halting and healing conflict?" To have an even greater impact, the interfaith movement must address a number of concerns.

Widening the Circle of Dialogue

1. *Traditionalists are welcome*

The dangers that threaten our world society may be the basis on which traditional members of the faiths may be encouraged to engage more fully in interfaith activity. Yet they are often put off by what they suppose to be the "liberal presuppositions" of the interfaith movement. There are those who reject any meeting with members of another faith tradition. Although these are often labeled "extremists" or "fundamentalists," the cause of their suspicion of and hostility to others may be primarily because of political and economic divisions. Many others who perhaps are best described as "traditionalists" do not wish to give religious legitimacy to another faith tradition. Quite possibly, they have not thought much about the matter, but do recognize that people of different faiths have to live together and therefore need to understand some basic things about each other: for example, what foods should not be served at a civic reception in a religiously plural city?

A pluralist society requires respect for those of other persuasions. Even societies where one religion is dominant may have to take account of significant religious minorities. Teddy Kollek, for example, while Mayor of Jerusalem, tried to be sensitive to the religious concerns of Muslim and Christian minorities. Many Islamic states have to make allowance for significant minorities of other faiths.

I doubt if we can reach widespread agreement on the philosophical or theological basis for interfaith work, at least in the immediate future. Perhaps rather than assuming that theological pluralism is the basis for interfaith dialogue, we should acknowledge a pluralism of dialogue. Probably within each religion one can find those to whom the labels "exclusivist," "inclusivist," and "pluralist" can be applied. Perhaps the need is to discover the contribution each group can make to interfaith dialogue.

For instance, the exclusivist stresses commitment, and this is a welcome reminder that interfaith activity should not evade questions of truth. The inclusivist speaks as a member of a particular faith community and can help that tradition reinterpret its theology so that while affirming its central witness it need not deny the witness of others. The pluralist acknowledges that the richness of the Divine Mystery cannot be contained in one tradition.

I wonder if even as individuals most of us operate within only one model. I recognize that in part I could fit under all the categories. I have a personal commitment as a disciple of Christ; in my theological thinking I seek as a Christian to see God's purpose in the whole religious life of humanity; and as a student of religion and as an interfaith activist, I do not presume that any faith has a privileged position.

2. Listening to Minority Voices

Practical cooperation is not without its difficulties. Is it genuinely inter-religious and international or are certain groups recruiting support for their own agenda? Marc Ellis in his *Unholy Alliance* reminds us that Palestinians feel that Christian-Jewish dialogue has added to their sufferings, while the Dalits in India feel this about Hindu-Christian dialogue.[6] In some places, women feel they have been excluded from the dialogue.

Does the emphasis on religious consensus allow space for the voices of religious minorities and of those who have no formal religious commitment? A consensus document may be a threat to minorities, especially to those whose religious identity is resented by the mainstream.

3. Listening to Spiritual Movements

We have also to recognize that spiritual wisdom is not the monopoly of religious officials. The Spirit, like the wind, "bloweth where it listeth." I believe that the Chicago Parliament did us all a good turn by opening its doors to all who wanted to come; on the whole, few religions have been in the vanguard of progress. Some groups did withdraw due to the inclusiveness, but that was their choice. It may well be that religious and denominational organizations and hierarchical leadership will become less significant in the next millennium.

4. Listening to Other Disciplines

Equally, we need the wisdom of the experts in many particular disciplines, especially those who are people of faith. Dialogue needs to be multi-disciplinary as well as multifaith. Experts in a whole range of disciplines may themselves be committed members of a faith. This was made clear to me when I spoke to the Retired Generals for Peace about the Global Ethic and the role of the military in peace-keeping. Many of those high-ranking officers were committed members of a faith.

If interfaith dialogue is to deal with the vital issues that face human society, it should not be confined to religious specialists or religious leaders. It needs to engage those with expertise in all the relevant disciplines. Particularly, there should be an attempt to involve in this debate those with political and economic power as well as those who control the media. They, however, will perhaps not be interested until there has been far wider public education about the vital importance of interfaith cooperation. Change will begin to happen only as the politically aware public demands that nations act in the interest of the world society and seek to shape that society according to ethical values upheld by the great spiritual traditions as well as by many humanists.

Difficulties to be Addressed

1. Disagreements Within Religions

We are all aware of the disagreements within religions. At one Christian-Jewish dialogue group, it was suggested after our first session that the Jews go into one room to sort out their differences and that the Christians should go into another and solve their disagreements. The differences may be not only theological, but relate to the great social, ecological, and moral issues which we have been suggesting should be the focus of interfaith activity.

Intra-religious dialogue is very important. But in our concern for the environment, the protection of human rights, and the struggle for economic justice, we may well find ourselves in opposition to some members of our own and other faiths. The more socially engaged the interfaith movement becomes, the less it may be a unifying force amongst all believers.

2. Interfaith Organizations Need To Work Together.

When people hear of another interfaith organization, the reaction may be, "Do we need another interfaith body?" To those on the outside, one interfaith group looks much the same as another, and the motley variety of initials used for the organizations seems designed to confuse.

In fact, there is plenty of work for them all to do. As we have seen, there is a great variety of approaches to interfaith work and each organization has its own particular focus and constituency. Only by working together will the interfaith movement be listened to by the media and by those who control economic and political power.

There have been suggestions that what is needed is a World Council of Faiths, which could perhaps be formed by the merging together of the various international interfaith organizations. It is questionable whether one super Organization would be more effective or just more bureaucratic. What seems to me important is a sense of partnership between the organizations and awareness of belonging to a movement that is bigger than any of us. I have hoped that there could be some coordinating body, rather like the International Council of Christians and Jews, for those engaged in Christian-Jewish dialogue, or the Society for Buddhist-Christian Studies.

The International Interfaith Centre (IIC) at Oxford, which has been set up by the International Association for Religious Freedom, the World Congress of Faiths, and Westminster College, Oxford, has as its purpose to encourage education about interfaith activity and to facilitate cooperation amongst all those engaged in this work. The Centre aims to hold information about interfaith work across the world, to keep those involved in touch with each other, while being a source of information to the media; it also aims to encourage research on questions of concern to many people involved in interfaith work, regardless of their particular organization.

As mentioned above, a particular concern at IIC conferences has been to examine how interfaith work can be more effective in areas of conflict, such as Sri Lanka, Northern Ireland, former Yugoslavia, and the Middle East. A series of programs on the overall theme "Community Building: Diverse Cultures in One Community" is being arranged. The center is also developing electronic communication capabilities. Nonetheless, hospitality to visitors to the Centre and the many individual contacts and introductions made by the Centre remain at the heart of its work to create a sense of spiritual fellowship amongst all engaged in what has been called a "Pilgrimage of Hope."

Wishful Thinking?

If the interfaith movement is to be effective in helping to rebuild our world on spiritual and moral principles, there is a great deal of work to be done. In many societies, religions are peripheral to the centers of economic and political power. Perhaps the greatest task is to argue that this is a moral and spiritual world.

Is that hope, as Hans Küng asks in his Preface to *A Global Ethic* (1993), a "sheer illusion"? In answer, as we have seen, he points "the eternal skeptic" to the worldwide change of awareness about economics and ecology, about world peace and disarmament, and about the partnership between men and women.[7]

Perhaps one special contribution of faith is to inspire hope that change is possible. Such a conviction is based on our inner life. Although I have stressed the needs of the world as our common agenda, the hope and energy to address this will come from the inner life of prayer and meditation. The source of practical action is our spirituality. Inner and outer belong together. The activist will be exhausted without an inner life and the true mystic longs for the world's renewal.

My hopes for interfaith work are graphically expressed in a passage at the end of Choan-Seng Song's *The Compassionate God*. There he described an African's dream of the world:

> A giant snake, enormously powerful, was coiling itself around the globe. The globe seemed too weak to withstand the pressure. I could see the first cracks in it. Then I saw a light at the center of the world. Enter into this light, I was told, but I resisted. . . But the light was irresistible. I went towards it and, as I did so, I saw many others moving towards it, too. And the snake's grip gradually began to loosen.

Choan-Seng Song comments on the dream:

> The world has in fact begun to crack. We seem destined for destruction at our own hands. But behold, miracle of miracles, out of the cracks a light shines. . . We all need that light, for that light is our only hope—we, the poor and the rich, the oppressed and the oppressors, the theists and the atheists, Christians, Muslims, Jews, Buddhists, and Hindus. We must all get to that light, for it is the light of love and life, the light of hope and the future. The movement of persons toward that light must have constituted a formidable power, for the snake, the demon, begins to loosen its grip on the globe.[8]

There is abundant spiritual energy and hope to release our world from the fears and dangers that threaten to crush us, if only we can harness that energy effectively.

NINE

Global Theology

The urgent needs of the world society are a compelling reason for religions to end their age-old rivalries and to work together for the common good. At a deeper level, the coming together of religions may lead also to a fuller awareness of the Divine.

Dr. Jonathan Sacks, as we have seen,[1] has argued powerfully from traditional Jewish sources for the importance of interfaith understanding. He stresses the plurality of religions. "Our moral and spiritual lives are as plural as languages."[2] He accepts that there are universal requirements of morality, but warns that both tribalism and universalism end in human sacrifice. Tribalism seeks to impose the identity of the tribe on others. Universalism does not allow for difference and plurality.

This is an attractive and powerful rationale for a minority faith. It puts mutual respect in the place of competitive mission. It allows a minority group to affirm its own identity without being a threat to others. Yet it suggests that, while there is a public world in which we live together, we each retreat home behind locked doors of faith. It is an argument that, for example, may be used to support educating children in separate religious schools. This may be good for their spiritual nurture, but may aggravate communal differences. Sacks' view also evades the question of whether our different understandings of the Divine are complementary or convergent.

Convergent Paths

For many pioneers of the interfaith movement, dialogue is a way in which we grow in our awareness of the Divine. Dr. S. Radhakrishnan, the distinguished Indian philosopher who became President of India and who was a patron of the World

Congress of Faiths, argued in his Kamala Lectures that in the new world society religions "are approximating to one another." The universal elements in them, he said, would be emphasized and "the gradual assimilation of religions will function as a world faith."[3] "The time has come," he wrote in his *Religion in a Changing World,* "for us to join in unity of spirit."[4] In a similar way, Professor Seshagiri Rao, who is the Editor of the forthcoming *Encyclopaedia of Hinduism,* in his 1982 Younghusband Lecture, said, "In the context of the emerging world community, all the great religions are useful, necessary, and complementary to one another as revealing different facets of the one Truth."[5] Dr. Robert Runcie, in his Younghusband lecture, quoted Paul Tillich that "in the depth of every living religion there is a point at which religion itself loses its importance, and that to which it points breaks through its particularity, elevating it to spiritual freedom and to a vision of the spiritual presence in other expressions of the ultimate meaning of man's existence."[6]

This approach rests on several assumptions. The first is a recognition of the relativity of all human language. Leonard Swidler, as we have seen, has argued that all statements about reality are conditioned by their author's historical setting, intention, culture, class, and sex. The limits of language are also recognized and it is seen that all knowledge is interpreted knowledge. Reality speaks to each person with the language he or she gives it. We are not in a position to make ultimate, unconditioned truth statements. Religious truth is communicated through symbols, metaphor, and poetry. Rituals and creeds point beyond themselves, whereas too often they have been given the authority that belongs only to God.[7]

Secondly, this recognition of the limits of language and human knowledge is also an affirmation of the Mystery of God who transcends our understanding. Pluralism, writes Stanley Samartha, an Indian theologian, is "the homage which the finite mind pays to the inexhaustibility of the infinite."[8] Bishop George Appleton spoke of "the mystery of the final Reality to whom or to which we give different names, so great and deep and eternal that we can never fully understand or grasp the mystery of Being."[9]

A third assumption of this approach is that God's concern is for every person and that, therefore, the insight and experience of each person is valuable. One may, in discussion, suggest that a person's views, while true to his or her experience, do not do justice to some experiences of other people. One may suggest that others have drawn wrong conclusions from their experience. There is room for debate and disagreement. But the dramatic change is from thinking that we have a truth, formulated in words and guaranteed correct by God, which is to be proclaimed and defended, instead of recognizing that each person's insight is of value. For me, in any case, belief in Jesus Christ is trust in a living person, but no person is fully encapsulated in words about them.

Others' Experience of the Divine is Authentic

If we begin to see that each person's deepest convictions are significant and an authentic experience of the Divine, we replace argument and hostility by respectful listening. His or her insight, like my own, is partial but nonetheless significant. This, I think, is what Swami Vivekananda was saying at the 1893 World's Parliament of Religions. He quoted from the *Bhagavad-Gita* that "Whosoever comes to Me, through whatsoever form, I reach him; all men are struggling through paths, which in the end lead to Me."[10] Later, he said of the Vedas that they are "without beginning and without end. But by the Vedas no books are meant. They mean the accumulated treasury of spiritual laws discovered by different persons in different times."[11] In the same way, a Christian's understanding of Jesus is shaped by the community of faith to which she or he belongs. There is also a Jewish saying that each Jew should write his own copy of the Torah scroll during his lifetime, which is sometimes taken to mean that each person has to work out his or her own faith.

The Religious Experience Research Unit, founded by Sir Alister Hardy, which has collected accounts of many peoples' religious experiences, has indicated what a wealth of religious experience there is to draw on. If we are willing to listen, we shall discover that many people have a treasured insight to share. Indeed, as I understand it, the Bible is the attempt of those met by God, particularly in the New Testament by God in Christ, to share that experience so that others might make it their own. Too often Christians have appeared to communicate truth about God, rather than inviting others to discover for themselves the divine love. As William Temple said in 1935, "revelation does not offer truth concerning God, but the Living God Himself."[12]

To accept as genuine the claims of a person of another faith to have been met by God is a major advance in interreligious understanding. There is an example of this in *Dialogue with a Difference,* a book arising from a Christian-Jewish dialogue group. At one point, Rabbi Tony Bayfield writes,

> What is it then that I feel compelled to say? It is this. I believe that many Christians find in the life and death of Jesus as described in the New Testament and in the tradition which flows from those events the fullest disclosures of the nature of God and God's will for them. Such faith involves no necessary error or illusion.[13]

Orthodox rabbi and scholar Irving Greenberg has said that God, whose love was already made known to Jews, reached out to make his love known to Gentiles through Christianity. "There is enough love in God to choose and to choose again."[14] In a similar way, a growing number of Christians now recognize that God's covenant with the Jewish people has never been abrogated.

The experience of the other that one accepts as a genuine experience of the Divine may not be the same as one's own experience. One may question the conclusions the other draws from his or her experience, yet its genuineness is acknowledged.

The Other's Experience is Significant for My Religious Life

Beyond this, however, may come the recognition not only that the experience of the other is genuine, but that it is religiously significant to me. Some time ago, the World Congress of Faiths invited Bishop Kenneth Cragg, a Christian scholar of Islam, to lead a conference about Islam. The intention was not only to describe Islam, but to help Christians to see the significance of Islam for their own religious lives.

Another example of the suggestion that the teachings of one faith are relevant to those of another may be found in Raimundo Panikkar's introduction to *The Vedic Experience*. Acknowledging that the Vedas are linked forever to the particular religious sources from which historically they spring, he suggests the Vedas are a monument of universal religious—and thus deeply human—significance. The anthology invites readers to appropriate the basic experience of Vedic Man, "not because it is interesting or ancient, but because it is human and thus belongs to us all."[15]

When Swami Vivekananda, who was himself an active reformer of Hinduism, said "we accept all religions as true," I doubt whether he meant that they are equally true, although critics have understood him in this sense. Rather, I think he was accepting that each person's experience was a genuine experience of God, however inadequate or misunderstood. This, I believe, gives a religious significance to dialogue. As we learn of the experiences of others, our own knowledge of the Divine is increased. As Rabindranath Tagore said, "To reject any part of humanity's religious experience is to reject truth."

Toward a World Theology

This leads toward both a world theology and shared spiritual exploration. In 1981, Wilfred Cantwell Smith wrote,

Henceforth the data for theology must be the data of the history of religions. The material on the basis of which a theological interpretation shall be proffered, of the world, man, the truth, and of salvation—of God and His dealings with His world—is to be the material that the study of the history of religion provides.[18]

Just as a Christian theologian reads the works of Christians of any denomination, so as we think about the great issues of life and death, we may draw upon the wealth of humankind's religious traditions. John Hick's book *Death and Eternal Life* is an example of this. In it, he tries to discover the insights enshrined in the various religious traditions of the world and to see how these different insights illuminate each other.

> Any writer on death and immortality is likely to start from within a particular religious tradition, which he either affirms or opposes, and within a particular historical culture. But if he restricts himself to the resources of his own religio-cultural milieu he will be interpreting the phenomenon of death from a restricted standpoint which is not warranted by the universality of the phenomenon itself. The experiences and reflections of all human faiths and cultures are relevant to the understanding of our mortality. This is par excellence a topic to which a trans-confessional and trans-cultural approach is appropriate.[19]

The fact that many Christians have been helped by Sogyal Rinpoche's *The Tibetan Book of Living and Dying* again indicates that this is a subject which is illuminated by a sharing of the insights of different traditions.[20]

This also proved to be the case at a weekend conference arranged several years ago by the World Congress of Faiths at which the theme was "Our Strength in Sorrow." People of different faith spoke of the resources they had found in their own tradition to help in times of difficulty. It was a time of deep personal sharing. Often participants discovered that they could find help in each others' traditions. John Bowker's *Problems of Suffering in Religions of the World* shows at a scholarly level that we may learn from the wisdom of each tradition as we ponder the mystery of suffering. "The realities of suffering are common to us all, and it is not hard to feel a very real identification with those who have expressed their feelings about this common experience—no matter what their time or place or generation may be."[21]

My work at the Council of Christians and Jews made me confront at a new depth the horror of the Holocaust. I became more aware of Christian complicity, through long centuries of anti-Jewish teaching, in the persecution and murder of Jews. I recognized also that the Shoah is a challenge to all, of whatever faith, who claim to believe in a God of love. In wrestling with this test of faith, I drew upon both Jewish and Christian resources. The question is not to members of one religion only nor can it be answered, if it can be answered at all, from the resources of one religious tradition alone.[22]

Not only do we need each other's wisdom as we reflect on central theological issues, we need to understand and make space for our disagreements. Already, for example, this is beginning to happen in Jewish-Christian dialogue. Christian and Jewish scholars, who have pioneered a new understanding of Judaism and the beginnings of Christianity in the first century of the common era, work together and are in large measure in agreement. Some Christian theologians are grappling with the question of how the Jewish "no" to Jesus is also within the purposes of God. For, as Friedrich-Wilhelm Marquardt has emphasized, "We will only have Christian anti-Judaism behind us when theologically we will have succeeded in making positive sense of the Jewish 'no' to Jesus."[23]

Similar developments are taking place in Christian-Buddhist dialogue. There has, for example, been quite a lot of mutual discussion about the Buddhist concept of Sunnyata or Emptiness and the Christian concept of Kenosis or the self-emptying of God in the incarnation of Jesus Christ.

A New Way of Doing Theology

Thirty years ago I visited Fr. Murray Roger's ashram in India.

Murray Rogers is one of the pioneers of the Christian attempt to enter deeply into the spiritual depths of other faiths. I recall that the Indian papers had a brief paragraph about John Robinson's *Honest to God,* which had just been published. I remember even more vividly being very moved that at the Eucharist, beside the expected readings from the Hebrew Bible and the New Testament, there were readings from the Vedas. The practice was maintained when the ashram moved to Jerusalem. I do not recall whether the reader said at the end of the lection from the Hindu scriptures, "This is the Word of the Lord." Yet the sort of global theology we are here envisaging suggests that authority belongs to all world scriptures.

The authority, however, is not so much that of a direct message from God but of the experience of those who have been met by the Divine. Dr. Radhakrishnan said of the Vedas that this is

> the accepted name for the highest spiritual truth of which the human mind is capable. It is the work of rishis or seers. . . . The rishis are not so much the authors of the truths recorded in the Vedas as the seers who were able to discern the eternal truths by raising their life spirit to the plane of the universal spirit. . . . They are the pioneer researchers in the realm of spirit who saw more in the world than their fellows. . . . When the Vedas are regarded as the highest authority, all that is meant is that the most exacting of all authorities is the authority of facts.[24]

For Christians, the Bible is the Word of God only in a secondary sense. It points beyond itself to the encounter with God which it records and invites the reader to be open to that same encounter. The Fourth Evangelist says, "These things are written that you may believe that Jesus is the Christ, the Son of God and that believing you may have life in his name."[25]

Scripture, indeed any creative writing, invites the reader to make his own the experience of the author. In our attempt to fathom the deep mysteries of life, we may learn from all spiritual explorers. We need to test their record by our own living experience of the Divine and it may be that some of the great saints only speak to us as we ourselves grow in sanctity. Theological study is changing from being the interpretation of an authoritative text to becoming an exploratory venture—the attempt to understand the mystery of life in the light of our own and other peoples' intuitions of the Ultimate.

Our thinking about the Ultimate needs to become an inter-religious search. As yet, interfaith dialogue is mostly still at the stage of explaining our beliefs to each other, if we have gotten that far. Perhaps by sharing and discussing those beliefs together we may not only have a "free and frank exchange of opinions," but move together to a deeper understanding of the Transcen-dent.

Yet because that Reality cannot be grasped by our intellects, we need to come together not only at the level of discussion, but also of prayer and meditation. The deepest meeting is in the "cave of the heart," which is the abode of the Spirit.

TEN

Global Spirituality

I doubt whether I would have started to reflect on Global Spirituality if I had not been been asked to write an article on this by Sister Vandana, who has a Christian ashram in the Himalayas. Like Bede Griffiths, she is a Christian who has entered deeply into Hindu spiritual traditions.

I have some hesitation about the word "spirituality." Just a couple of days before writing this chapter there was an article in the London *Times* about the current American craze for spirituality. It ends with the comment that, in contrast, "the British as a nation are slightly embarrassed about it. The media don't write about it, publishers don't talk about it and booksellers won't admit to the success of the spiritual section hidden on the third floor."[1] The late Donald Nicholl speaks too of a sense of embarrassment both about writing or reading a book called *Holiness*. It is not something you want to be seen reading in public.[2]

The term also can have a wide meaning. The *Times* article lumps together books "featuring the care of the soul, near-death experiences, encounters with angels, personal spiritual growth and pocket-sized thoughts for the day." In my understanding the word means the wish to open oneself (or perhaps better to be opened) to the Divine and to be shaped by the Divine. This includes the ultimate longing to see God and the hope to be made into the likeness of Christ. The Prayer of Humble Access in the Anglican Communion Service includes the words "that we may evermore dwell in him (Christ) and he in us." The yearning is for one's will to become obedient to the loving purposes of God. My hesitation with the word "spirituality" is that it may suggest "holy feelings" or a special spiritual state of consciousness. This may be granted to some, but in my view such experiences are the gift of God and not to be directly sought.

A further hesitation is that spiritual experiences are not an end in themselves but are given to equip a person to serve others. Mahatma Gandhi wrote,

> Man's ultimate aim is the realization of God, and all his activities, social, political, religious, have to be guided by this ultimate aim of the vision of God. The immediate service of all human beings, *sarvodaya*, becomes a necessary part of the endeavour, simply because the only way to find God is to see him in his creation and to be one with it. I am part and parcel of humanity. . . . If I could persuade myself that I could find him in a Himalayan cave, I would proceed there immediately. But I know that I cannot find him apart from humanity.[3]

Vivekananda, earlier, had dedicated himself to "My God, the poor of all races."[4]

It is remarkable that so many of the people who have had a creative influence on this century have been men or women of spiritual vision. For me, the longing for spiritual growth is a part of the concern for the renewal of the world. As Thomas Merton said, "In solitude, in the depths of a man's aloneness, lie the resources for resistance to injustice."[5] My hesitation with the word "spirituality" is partly because it may suggest an isolation from the world rather than empowerment to struggle for peace and justice.

* * * * *

The particular question I want to consider here is how far a person of one religious tradition may enter into the spiritual depth of another tradition. Can a Christian feel as a Hindu does in prayer? Are we in separate worlds or can we as a guest enter another's spiritual home. If we can, how are we enriched by this experience? Are we still at home in one particular family of faith or has "interfaith" in fact become a new spiritual path? If it has not, is it nonetheless appropriate at times for people of different faiths to pray together?

Are There Varieties Of Mystical Experience?

I have long been fascinated by the claim of Sri Ramakrishna, a Hindu seer of the last century, that by following different spiritual paths, he reached the same spiritual realization. As a young man he was a devotee at the temple of the Divine Mother, Kali, in Calcutta. After an agonizing time of waiting, he realized the presence of the Divine Mother. A little later he focused his attention on Rama and had the same spiritual experience. Later, he followed the path of Advaita, then both the Muslim and Christian paths and had visions of the prophet and of Christ.[6]

Once when I visited a Sikh ashram near Delhi, as I was talking to the receptionist, she said, "I keep praying to Christ but still he does not grant me a vision." At the ashram, there was a place that visitors were shown where the guru had received such a vision. The Christian, however, might feel that this only showed that Christ had been absorbed into the Indian pantheon.

This sense of an underlying unity of mystical experience was reflected, at the 1893 World's Parliament of Religions, in Swami Vivekananda's call for tolerance. "To the Hindu," he said, "the whole world of religions is only a travelling, a coming up of different men and women through various conditions and circumstances to the same goal."[7]

There has been considerable academic discussion about the nature of mystical experience, whether it is essentially the same or whether there are different types of experience. There has also been the attempt of those deeply committed to one faith to enter into the spiritual experience of those of another. Swami Abhishiktananda, Fr. Bede Griffiths, and members of the Inter-Monastic Council have pioneered this. Buddhist monks have spent time in Christian monasteries and Christians have spent time at monasteries in Japan and Thailand. The World Congress of Faiths has arranged weekends of meditation led by members of different faiths in the hope of discovering where we meet in the Spirit.

Can We Stand With Others When They Pray?

This exploration is not easy. David Brown, a former Bishop of Guildford and a Christian scholar of Islam, wrote once that

> My distance from Islam came home to me in a sad but profound way one evening in Khartoum, when I went to the home of a Muslim religious leader. There were some thirty men sitting at ease in his courtyard, and for an hour or more we enjoyed a good and open discussion about religious matters. Then the time came for the night prayer and they formed ranks to say it together. I asked if I might stand with them but the Sheikh told me I could not do so, since I did not have the right 'intention.' I had to remain standing at the edge of the courtyard. Even though I have walked on the approaches of Islam for over thirty years, I can only speak of it as a stranger.[8]

I felt something of this distance at an ashram at the Hindu pilgrimage town of Rishikesh. It was early in the morning. I had observed the *puja* or worship of, and offerings to, the gods. Then I had joined the monks in their meditation. Suddenly the lights were turned out and I had an overwhelming sense of the darkness, the nothingness of God. I know that Christian mystics speak of such experiences, but I felt I was in an alien world.

The life of faith is nourished in a particular faith community. Such a community has its beliefs, its symbols, its pattern of worship, its expected behavior. These are interwoven and cannot easily be unraveled. There is a particularity about the life of faith. To what extent are we able to enter into another tradition's spiritual experience or do we impose our own meaning on it? This is partly a question of understanding the other at depth but also of whether another's spiritual occasion can become for us an encounter with the Divine.

At a recent conference in India, I noted that the Roman

Catholic participants were very ready to go to and join in Hindu devotional services—happily chanting the *Bhajans*. I asked some of them about this and their answer was that mentally they addressed this praise to Jesus.

On the other hand in Japan, my wife Mary and I were guests with some others at a Shinto shrine. We were invited to share in the *misogi* ritual. This involves, at night time, standing under a waterfall. It is an act of purification and oneness with nature. Rev. Yamamoto, who revived the shrine, practised the ritual every night for ten years, to purify his country and the shrine from the abuses of militarism and war. I had not felt well that day and was more concerned about whether I would cope with the cold water. Mary, however, said she had indeed this sense of oneness. Covered with the pouring water, the boundaries between the body and nature seemed to dissolve. This seems to have been a Shinto experience and not what she would usually feel at a Christian service of communion.

I can think of one such experience when I was asked to attend a ritual conducted by an African religious leader. I had felt depressed beforehand, but as I took part I sensed the joy of life and of God. Three other occasions stand out in my memory. Once, in British Columbia, we were asked to stand by a beautiful lakeside and observe a ceremony conducted by a native Canadian spiritual leader. As she led us in prayer, I began to sense a spiritual presence in nature. This reflected the native Canadian feeling of being part of the natural world, which is alive with the one spirit of God. The second occasion was at a conference at which I was invited to take part in a Shinto ritual by offering branches of a tree. Again, it helped me to a deeper reverence for nature. A third occasion was a visit to the Western Wall in Jerusalem. I had been there two or three times as a tourist, but late one evening I went with a Jewish friend whose father was very ill. As we stood there she slipped a small paper, with a prayer on it, between the stones. The place became to me for the first time a holy place, a place of prayer.

In a similar way, many people have found the scriptures and

prayers of other faith traditions inspiring. A number of devotional books have an interfaith character. The *Oxford Book of Prayer*, for example, includes prayers from several traditions as does the *Lotus Prayer Book*.[9]

Is "Interfaith" Only Another Path?

At one point in his Reith Lectures, Dr. Jonathan Sacks says

A multicultural mind can use Zen for inwardness, Hassidic tales for humour, liberation theology for politics, and nature mysticism for environmental concern. But that is a little like gluing together slices of da Vinci, Rembrandt, Van Gogh, and Picasso and declaring the result a composite of the best in western art.[10]

As I have said, each religious tradition has its own integrity and I am not suggesting such pasting together. But if we have been shaped by and treasure Western music, may we not also learn to appreciate the beauties of Indian music? Indeed there are now musical works which draw upon both traditions. Can we not admire both the great Gothic cathedrals of Western Europe and the mosques of India? I believe that just as we can come to speak a language that is not our native tongue or appreciate a culture that is not our own, so we can to some extent enter the spiritual life of another faith community. Because this is the heart of the religious life, it is the most vital aspect of interreligious fellowship, even if it is the most sensitive. Here we begin to appreciate the other in the depths of his or her spirituality.

"Take off your shoes, for the place where you are standing is holy ground."[11] God's words to Moses are a warning to all who approach the sanctuary of another faith. There is much that we shall not understand: the sacred language, the mythology, the music, the age-old gestures and ritual movements. Yet if we believe in the Oneness of God and the unity of the human family, then despite all the splendid difference and variety, there is "the selfsame aching" for God in every human heart. The attempt to enter sympathetically into the spiritual life of other traditions is a vital contribution to human unity, for such meeting is at the deepest level of our being.

It may be also that not only do we begin to appreciate the other's spirituality, but that our own also is enriched. While our regular spiritual diet will continue to be that of our faith community, it will be deepened by our discoveries, just as many peoples' traditional meals have been added to by dishes from overseas. There are some who draw from several spiritual traditions, but do not count themselves members of any particular faith community—some call themselves seekers or even universalists.

There are in North America "interfaith" ministers. I remember also meeting someone who had described himself on his name-label as a "Hindu-Christian." That is not the path for me. I feel it is rootedness that gives the security for openness. My meeting with those of other faiths has been as a disciple of Jesus Christ. But we should expect variety here. While the majority of members of the World Congress of Faiths have been committed members of a particular faith, there have always been some members who call themselves "seekers." We may also hope to learn from the experience of people of different faith who marry each other and also from the children of such "interfaith" homes.

Together

Whatever our background and approach, there are moments when the gift of togetherness blinds us to our labels. At the Assisi World Day of Prayer for Peace, the purpose, in the official language, was "to be together to pray." For some, at least, it was an experience of "praying together." In some interfaith services that I have attended or helped to arrange there has been an experience of oneness felt by almost everyone present. At one service, held at Christ Church, Bath, we invited the readers to select a passage from their tradition about forgiveness and reconciliation. These were not texts from sacred writings but stories which told of recent experiences. As we listened together, the sources of the stories did not matter, for their messages spoke to us all.

I recall two recent occasions when people of faith came together to remember the victims of cruel death. One was at the Argentine Chancery in London, when Jews, Christians, and Muslims remembered those who had died in the bombing in Buenos Aires on July 18th, 1994. Soon afterwards, I shared in the Nagasaki Day Pilgrimage from Westminster Cathedral to the Peace Pagoda in Battersea Park. There, as people of many faiths (and it made for a long occasion!) offered prayers for peace, there was a unity in our longing that such horror should never be repeated. My mind went back a few months to a visit to Hiroshima, where with some Buddhists, one of whom was a survivor, we were silent together in prayer and remembrance.

Interfaith worship attracts strong opposition because it is the most powerful symbolic expression of the interfaith vision. Symbols always speak more eloquently than words. As long ago as 1952, the psychologist Professor Thoules told the World Congress of Faiths that arranging interfaith services might well be the best way of forwarding the aims of the Congress. Interfaith worship is not a substitute for the regular life of prayer and worship of a particular faith community, but it is a powerful symbolic reminder of our unity in the presence of the Holy One. In the Bible, all people are said to be descended from common ancestors, namely Adam and Eve. If we are to live together in one world, we need to recognize that we are one family, children of One God.[12]

ELEVEN

One World Faith?

I ended my first book, *Together to the Truth*, with these words:

> One world faith will emerge by a process of reconception. As the great religions respond to the world in which they live and to each other, so their fundamental insights will develop and broaden. This is quite different from an easy and artificial amalgam of diverse creeds. It is the growing together of living, developing organisms. As a Christian, I believe that Christ will stand at the centre of the emerging world faith.[1]

Twenty five years later, I retain this vision but would want to word it more carefully. Although I disowned a wish to see an artificial amalgam of creeds, it is clear that this is what the term "one world faith" suggests to most people, just as the word "syncretism" is usually used in a pejorative sense.

It would be better to speak of a growing recognition that people of all faiths share a common quest. They seek the One Ultimate reality who is forever seeking them. This common quest is shown by the growing together of the life of the religious communities of the world, although this is often resisted, sometimes violently, by extremists. It is reflected in the beginnings of global theology, global ethics, and global spirituality.

This sense of a common quest, in which differences should be valued, should help to overcome the hostility and rivalry still so evident between many members of different faiths. It should also inspire people of all faiths to work together for a world of peace and justice where all people enjoy the fullness of life and in which all of the natural world is cherished.

I recognize now that the way in which I spoke of Christ twenty-five years ago was too defensive. It is my very faith in

Christ, who reveals the unbounded love of God for all people, that has impelled me to a universalist vision.

Reconception

Together to the Truth was based on William Hocking's theory of "reconception." It was an attempt to test out his thesis of reconception by comparing developments within Christianity and Hinduism since the early nineteenth century. W. E. Hocking was an American philosopher who chaired the American Laymen's report *Rethinking Missions, a Laymen's Enquiry after a Hundred Years* (1932). The Commission traveled widely and the report's factual observations are still interesting. Controversy surrounded the summary, which was mostly the work of Hocking. The task of the missionary today (i.e. in the thirties), the report suggested, was to see what was good in other religions and to help their adherents to recover the best elements of their own faiths. The ultimate aim of missionary work, in so far as the report articulated one, seems to have been the emergence of the various religions out of isolation into a world fellowship in which each would find its appropriate place.

Hocking developed these ideas in two longer works: *Living Religions and a World Faith* and *The Coming World Civilization*. He argued that the whole trend of global life is towards unity and community of outlook, and that therefore there is a need for a single world religion. How, he then asked, might a Christian work for such a world-faith? One method was "radical displacement"—the replacement of other world religions by Christianity so that the whole world becomes Christian. This, it is probably fair to say, was the traditional missionary hope, as shown for example in the slogan "the world for Christ in our generation." The second method he suggested was "synthesis," which would include the adoption of some ceremonial and ideas from other traditions into Christianity. This seems to have been, for example, the position of John Henry Barrows, who was the Chairman of the 1893 World's Parliament of Religions. He wrote at one point, "The idea of evolving a cosmic or universal faith out of the Parliament was not present in the minds of its chief promoters. They believed that the elements of such religion are already contained in the Christian ideal and Christian scriptures."[2] In his Barrows lecture, which he gave in Asia, Henry Barrows further explained why he believed that Christianity was destined to become the universal religion of the entire world. He based his argument on an evolutionary theory of religion, whereby "lower" forms of religion are absorbed into "higher" religion. Eventually these higher religions will be assimilated to the religion of Christ. Christianity, he claimed, was "a celestial seed capable of indefinite expansion and wide variation."[3]

The third method, which Hocking himself favored, is "reconception." Suppose two religions partly overlap in their teaching or practice. In the way of synthesis the one will reach over and try to include part of the other: but members of the other religion will not agree about what is "inessential." In the process of reconception, a religion does not lose its shape, but expands as its growth in understanding increases. Religions are continually growing or rethinking as they come in contact with new people and ideas. At any one stage a religion is a complete and shapely whole: but it is also in constant need of reconception.

In part the current need for reconception is in response to contemporary intellectual developments. For example, the work of Darwin, Einstein, and subsequent thinkers has made it necessary for religions to reformulate their teaching about the beginning of the world. Advances in genetical studies are causing a similar rethinking about the beginnings of life. Awareness of living in a multi-religious world has caused members of many faiths to re-consider their teaching about the attitude of their faith to that of others. The decree of the Second Vatican Council, *Nostra Aetate*, is an example of such rethinking in the Roman Catholic Church, but, significantly, a rethinking that appealed to and based itself on traditional teaching.

Because now more than ever all religions live in the same

world, they all have to respond to the same intellectual challenges—including secularism and technological advances. There is often a willingness to distinguish that which is inessential, because shaped by particular histories and cultures, from that which is at the heart of a tradition. The responses of religions to common stimuli mean that to some extent as they change, the common elements become clearer. The argument of my *Together to the Truth* is that the evidence of the last two centuries does indicate that the reconception which has taken place within the world religions has also brought religions closer together.

Reasons to Expect a World Faith

There are other reasons for expecting a coming world faith, if we use that term to mean the growing sense of a fellowship of all believers. The gradual emergence of a world society seems to require some shared spiritual values. In 1939 Sarvepalli Radhakrishnan asked: "Should we not give a spiritual basis to the world which is now being mechanically made to feel its oneness by modern scientific inventions?"[4] More recently, the Duke of Edinburgh, in his Preface to Hans Küng's *Global Responsibility*, comments, "While it has proved possible to arrive at a broad consensus about the facts of life on earth, so far at least, it has proved impossible to overcome the jealousies, rivalries and the destructive consequences of competing religions and ideologies."[5] The feeling for a world faith rests also on a belief that the coming together of peoples in a global society is under the guidance of the Divine Spirit. This reflects a Biblical belief that however ambiguous history may seem it is, nevertheless, the sphere of God's operation.

This emerging world society is bringing together the diverse histories of traditionally separate faith communities. The "provincialism" of so much of our knowledge was brought home to me when I attended a *Son et Lumière* at the Red Fort in Delhi. Although my degree was in history, here we listened to the history of Emperors of whom I had scarcely heard. No one had noticed that my course ignored the history of whole continents.

Religious thinking was carried on in similar isolation. Now, gradually, members of one faith are becoming aware of the history, teaching and writings of other great religions. This is making possible the emergence of world theology.[6]

The urgency of the crises that confront humanity is another compelling reason to encourage religious people to work together. Practical cooperation for peace and human welfare has helped many people of faith discover a sense of oneness. Archbishop Angelo Fernandes, for example, has described the World Conference on Religion and Peace as "trying to create a unity of conscience or, if you prefer, a universal conscience around the basic convictions shared by all living faiths."[7] Again, it was the critical issues facing humankind that was the focus of shared concern at the 1993 Chicago Parliament and to which, as we have considered, the Declaration *Toward a Global Ethic* was a response.[8]

The feeling for an emerging world faith also reflects the view that the Mystery of the Ultimate transcends our pictures and doctrines and that, therefore, each person's experience of the Ultimate is relevant to us all. Stanley Samartha has written, "A sense of Mystery provides a point of unity to all plurality. In a pluralistic world, the different responses of different religions to the Mystery of the Infinite or *Theos* or *Sat* need to be acknowledged as valid."[9] A number of writers speak of convergence. This is why dialogue at its deepest is truth seeking—Global Theology. It is not just a matter of understanding the other nor certainly of avoiding disagreement but of entering into a search for deeper truth which draws upon the spiritual heritage of all people. For this reason, I believe that, as I have already argued, the attempt to enter into the spiritual experience of other traditions, sometimes referred to as "global spirituality," and interfaith worship have a creative contribution to make to our mutual understanding.

A Common Quest

I do not think that at some future point it will be possible to draw up a world creed. This is why it seems better to speak of a common quest or a shared pilgrimage rather than of an emerging "one world religion." This is partly because there will be new questions and challenges, partly because variety itself is to be valued, and partly because there will always be more to learn about Ultimate Reality.

Durwood Foster, a Professor of Theology at Berkeley, writing of what he calls "ultimology" or a "universal theology" has this sense of the goal always being on the horizon.

> Ultimology in every tradition, I believe, in this sense of committed quest, must strive for universality. It will never reach it, as Kipling suggests, short of the great Judgment Seat. Its trajectory is asymptotic, with many dips and squiggles. It is a regulative ideal, in Kant's sense. Like perfection, as John Wesley understood it, it is something to be going on toward, not something a right-headed ultimology will ever claim for itself.[10]

My picture is of the religious history of humankind becoming one history. It is largely true that Christian theology is no longer denominational theology. In considering a theological issue, most students will read those who have made significant contributions to the subject, regardless of their denomination. In the same way, we shall increasingly draw upon insights from the great religious traditions. We need, as Durwood Foster says, "to be really encountered in mind and heart by the truth of the other, without being able either to dismiss it or subsume it under one's own truth."[11]

This sense that the goal is always on the horizon may in part meet Raimundo Panikkar's questioning of the assumption of underlying or ultimate unity that seems to be presupposed by those who speak of convergence. He distinguishes pluralism from plurality. "Pluralism," he says, "means something more than sheer acknowledgment of plurality and the mere wishful thinking of unity."[12] He continues: "Pluralism does not consider unity an indispensable ideal. . . nor is it the eschatological expectation that in the end all shall be one."[13] Pluralism recognizes that Being is not fully apprehended by human thought. It rejects "the monotheistic assumption of a totally intelligible Being" and "makes us aware of our own contingency/limitations and nontransparency of reality."[14]

The Japanese scholar, Masao Abe, also rejects the search for a common denominator.

> Each religion is fully realized in its distinctiveness, and yet it is critically judged by the other religions, as well as by itself in the light of its encounter with other religions. It is beyond the polarity of the affirmative and negative stances and is realized through the realization that there is no common denominator for world religions. A positionless position makes other positions possible through establishing a dynamic harmony among the world religions, and opening up the dynamic unity in the religious pluralism of our time.[15]

The Mystery is not fully grasped by human understanding. We have to beware of searching for a universal system, lest our theological agreement becomes an idol in place of the Living Mystery. What we can do is recognize and joyfully affirm that people in every great religious tradition seek and are met by that One Reality. This is why dialogue is not only personally enriching but helps to create a spiritual fellowship in which we recognize the bonds of our common humanity even while we acknowledge that our response to the Mystery is expressed in very different pictures, symbols and intellectual systems.

The "one world faith" of which I wrote twenty-five years ago was modeled too much on pictures of the universal church. I extrapolated ideas from then current Christian ecumenical thinking and tried to apply them to the wider ecumenical movement among religions. My picture now is that of a pilgrimage. Each year in London a multi-faith pilgrimage is held. This has several starting points, but gradually the pilgrims converge on one shrine. I rather suspect that in this pilgrimage the shrine will always recede into the distance.

Bede Griffiths' Vision

I first entered into correspondence with Fr. Bede Griffiths in the late 1960's while preparing to write *Together to the Truth*. Later, his *A New Vision of Reality* prompted me to look again at what I had written in *Together to the Truth*. In the final chapter of this, his last book, Fr. Griffiths speaks of rediscovering "the perennial philosophy, the traditional wisdom, which is found in all religions and especially in the great religions of the world." Members of the Semitic religions, he insists, will have to give up their exclusive claims. "This would free them to recognise the action of God in all humanity from the beginnings of history." Christian theology, he points out, evolved in Europe. "We have to look forward to a theology which would evolve in contact with Hindu, Buddhist, Taoist and Confucian thought and at the same time a liturgy which would develop from contact with the art, music and dance of Asian and African peoples." One characteristic of the new culture, he says, would be its feminine aspects.[18] "We have now reached the limit of this masculine culture with its aggressive, competitive, rational, analytic character."

Bede Griffiths ends his book like this:

> The only way of recovery is to rediscover the perennial philosophy, the traditional wisdom, which is found in all ancient religions and especially in the great religions of the world. But those religions have in turn become fossilized and have each to be renewed, not only in themselves but also in relation to one another, so that a cosmic, universal religion can emerge, in which the essential values of Christian religion will be preserved in living relationship with the other religious traditions of the world. This is a task for the coming centuries as the present world order breaks down and a new world order emerges from the ashes of the old.[19]

I have three questions about this passage, which in so many ways resonates with my own thinking. Is it only a rediscovery of the perennial philosophy that we need? This takes away the sense of newness about the insights we are discovering, as we relate the inherited wisdom of the great religions to the amazing advances in so many fields of human intellectual endeavour. Bede Griffiths partly recognizes this himself when he says that the religions have become fossilized. Secondly, I have already questioned what the phrase "a cosmic universal religion" might mean. My third question relates to the phrase "in which the essential values of Christian religion can emerge," although this is not so triumphalistic as my own sentence of twenty-five years ago that "As a Christian, I believe that Christ will stand at the centre of the emerging world faith."

Christ Calls Us To Serve God's Kingdom

A rabbi and good friend balked at a sentence in the final section of Paul Knitter's *No Other Name?* where Knitter writes, "Perhaps Jesus the Nazarene will stand forth (without being imposed) as the unifying symbol, the universally fulfilling and normative expression, of what God intends for all history." The rabbi felt that Christian superiority had been smuggled in by the back door to a book that is a plea for pluralism. Knitter, however, continues,

> In carrying on the dialogue among religions, however, Christians must bear in mind that if such a recognition of Jesus does eventually result from the praxis of dialogue, it will be a "side effect" of the dialogue. Whether the question of Jesus' uniqueness is answered, whether Jesus does or does not prove to be final and normative, is not, really, the central issue or the primary purpose of dialogue. The task at hand, demanded of Christianity and all religions by both the religious and the socio-political world in which they live, is that religions speak and listen to each other, that they grow with and from each other, that they combine efforts for the welfare, the salvation, of all humanity. If this is being done, then the central hopes and goals of all religions will be closer to being realized. Allah will be known and praised; the Lord Krishna will act in the

world; enlightenment will be furthered and deepened; God's kingdom will be understood and promoted.[21]

For whose sake does the Christian slip into a universalist vision a plea for the superiority of Jesus? Surely not for the one who did "not prize his equality with God, but who humbled himself, assuming the nature of a slave."[22] To picture Jesus and Mohammed and the Buddha and others competing for a prize for their contribution to "progress in religion" is at once to see the absurdity of the suggestion. Jesus' own message centered on the coming kingdom of God. For those who follow Jesus the longing and indeed daily prayer is that God's kingdom will come on earth as it is in heaven. Jesus defined that kingdom as good news for the poor, release for the prisoner, recovery of sight for the blind, freedom for the victims of cruelty. The ultimate picture and hope is of a world at peace, a world of justice where all share God's gift of abundant life. It is not, despite well-known Christian hymns with splendid tunes, a coronation ceremony.

Hans Ucko, of the World Council of Churches Office for Inter-Religious Relations, writes that

> Jews and Christians, though in different ways, are both wait-ing for the Messiah to come. . . . There is a story about a Jew and a Christian engaged in heated discussion. All of a sudden someone comes in and says: "We hear that the Messiah is coming." They run to the place where the Messiah is to appear. And there he is. They both go up to him and ask: "Is this your first or second visit?" The Messiah responds: "No comment." The story doesn't end there. It goes on to say, "Perhaps now you will understand the true meaning of the Messiah: messianism is the quality of life that we live together along the way."[23]

God's will is abundant life for all people. Jesus came to proclaim and embody that good news of life in all its fullness. Members of the church are those who identify with Jesus' vision of abundant life and seek to promote God's reign of love.

All who also seek that goal are to be welcomed as allies. As a student in India, I used to help at a clinic for leprosy patients. One day I walked there with two other students. One was a Muslim from Tamilnad and the other a Christian from Sri Lanka. The doctor at the clinic was a devotee of the Hindu god Siva. We were together in service of those in need who ministered to us by their cheerfulness. Now, the urgency of interfaith cooperation in a world of violence and suffering has become ever more apparent.

As we cooperate, we discover that we are impelled to do so by the deepest convictions of our particular faith. Twenty-five years ago when I spoke sympathetically of a coming world faith, I was made to feel by fellow Christians that I was betraying Christ. It is, however, my commitment to Christ that has impelled me to work for interfaith understanding and cooperation. The God whom I see revealed in Jesus Christ is a God of boundless love whose mercy is for all people. God seeks to break down barriers and to reconcile men and women both to himself and to each other. God shares the suffering of the homeless and the hungry and appeals to the conscience of the world through the cries of the refugee and the victims of torture. "For Christians," writes Durwood Foster, "Jesus Christ is the centre we are coming from, but he is an eccentric centre, a self-transcending centre, an outward impelling centre."[24]

My hope for an emerging world faith does not make me feel any less a Christian. For me the various titles of Jesus and the doctrine of the incarnation are primarily ways of saying that in Jesus Christ I, like millions of other people, have been met by God. That others have encountered Divine Reality through other bearers of truth does not lessen the reality of my own experience of the all-accepting, self-giving love of God made known in Jesus Christ. I recognize that others will use very different language to express their convictions. My use of personal and theistic terms indicates that Jesus Christ is the center from which I am coming. If that to which the Christian is committed is found to be similar to that to which followers of other faiths are committed, this is a matter for rejoicing. My commitment to Christ is a commitment to what I believe to be true.

When Rolf Hochhuth's play *The Representative,* which was critical of Pope Pius XII's alleged acquiescence with the Nazis, was first produced, Pope John XXIII was asked what one should do about the play. "Do?" he replied, "What can one do about the truth?"[25] If, as I believe, in Christ I have been encountered by the truth, I do not doubt that he and his message will be of continuing significance. Presumably followers of other great faiths would say the same of their core convictions. My hope, while continuing to be a disciple of Christ, is that I might also begin to become a follower of the Buddha, learn from God's word in the Qur'an and the Torah and sense the oneness taught long ago by the rishis of India.

"There's a Dream I Feel"

The closer we come to the Holy One, the less labels matter. The English mystic Evelyn Underhill said that religions meet where religions take their source—in God. As a Sufi poet said long ago,

On my way to the Mosque, Oh Lord, I passed the Magian in front of his flame, deep in thought, and a little further I heard a rabbi reciting his holy book in the synagogue, and then I came upon the church where the hymns sung gently in my ears and finally I came into the mosque and pondered how many are the different ways to You—the one God.[26]

"The function of a religion," John Hick has written, is

to bring us to a right relationship with the ultimate divine reality, to awareness of our true nature and our place in the Whole, into the presence of God. In the eternal life there is no longer any place for religions; the pilgrim has no need of a way after he has finally arrived. In St. John's vision of the heavenly city at the end of our Christian scriptures it is said that there is no temple—no Christian church or chapel, no Jewish synagogue, no Hindu or Buddhist temple, no Muslim mosque, no Sikh gurdwara. . . . For all these exist in time, as ways through time to eternity.[27]

My ultimate vision, then, is of a growing awareness among people of all faiths that they are embarked upon a common quest. As they share with others their inherited spiritual treasures and their own experiences, their sense of the beauty and love and wonder of the Divine will grow. At the same time they will be more deeply moved to work for the coming of God's kingdom in which all people enjoy the gift of life in a world without war and poverty, where the life of every being is valued and respected.

A world in agony desperately needs the hope and transforming action that, together, people of faith can offer. I'm reminded of an end-of-term Assembly at the Primary School in Marsh Baldon, where we live; the children had chosen one of their favorite songs.

> There's a dream I feel, so rare, so real,
> All the world in union, the world as one.

> Gathering together one mind, one heart;
> Ev'ry creed, ev'ry colour once joined, never apart.
> It's the world in union, the world as one;
> As we climb to reach our destiny, a new age has begun.[28]

I'm also reminded of the opening ceremony for the Year of Inter-religious Understanding and Cooperation, when children from Barham Junior School, dressed as doctors and nurses, tended a sick world. One child with a stethoscope listened to the globe and called out "Quick, its dying." The other children then began to help and to sing Michael Jackson's song "Heal the world."

My faith is that in a global age the spiritual riches of the great religions will inspire children of all faiths to act together to heal the world. As a seven-year-old Spanish child has said, "We would be much happier if we learn to speak and to listen; if we know how to get along with each other; if we could trust each other."[29]

Resources

For Further Reading

World Religions

Beversluis, Joel, (ed.) *A SourceBook for Earth's Community of Religions,* CoNexus Press (with CPWR, 1993); Revised Edition with Global Education Associates, 1995 (see address below)

Bowker, John, *The Oxford Dictionary of World Religions,* Oxford University Press, 1997

Clarke, Peter B., *The World's Religions: Understanding the Living Faiths,* Reader's Digest 1993

Fisher, Mary Pat and Luyster, Robert, *Living Religions: An Encyclopedia of the World's Faiths,* I.B.Tauris, 1990 and Revised 2nd Edtn 1996

Anthologies

Braybrooke, Marcus, and Jean Potter, (eds.) *All in Good Faith: A Resource Book for Multi-faith Prayer,* World Congress of Faiths, Oxford 1997 and available in North America from CoNexus Press

Griffiths, Bede, (ed.) *Universal Wisdom,* HarperCollins 1994

Andrew Wilson, (ed.)*World Scripture: A Comparative Anthology of Sacred Texts,* Paragon House, New York 1991

Interfaith History

Braybrooke, Marcus, *Pilgrimage of Hope: One Hundred Years of Global Interfaith Dialogue,* Crossroad, New York, and SCM, London 1992

Seager, Richard Hughes,(ed.) *The Dawn of Religious Pluralism: Voices from the World's Parliament of Religions,* 1893, Open Court, Chicago 1993

Storey, Celia and David, *Visions of an Interfaith Future: Proceedings of Sarva-Dharma-Sammelana,* Bangalore 1993; International Interfaith Centre, Oxford 1994

Teasdale, Wayne and Cairns, George (eds), *The Community of Religions: Voices and Images of the Parliament of the World's Religions (1993),* Continuum, New York 1996

Global Ethic

Braybrooke, Marcus, (ed.) *Stepping Stones to a Global Ethic,* Crossroad, New York, and SCM, London 1992

Küng, Hans, *Global Responsibility,* Continuum, New York 1993

Küng, Hans and Kuschel, Karl-Josef, *A Global Ethic,* Continuum, New York and SCM Press, London 1993

Küng, Hans, (ed.) *Yes to a Global Ethic,* Continuum, New York 1996 and SCM in the UK, London 1996.

Key Issues

Knitter, Paul, *One Earth, Many Religions,* Orbis 1996

Samartha, Stanley, *One Christ–Many Religions,* Orbis 1991

Useful Addresses

Braybrooke Press, c/o Marcus Braybrooke, Marsh Baldon Rectory, Oxford OX44 9LS UK

Center for World Thanksgiving, Thanks-Giving Square, PO Box 1770, Dallas, TX 75221 USA

CoNexus Press, c/o Joel Beversluis, P.O. Box 6902, Grand Rapids, MI 49516 USA; *email:* conexus@iserv.net

Council for a Parliament of the World's Religions, PO Box 1630, 105 W. Adams, Suite 800, Chicago, IL 60690-1630 USA

International Association for Religious Freedom (IARF), 2 Market Street, Oxford OXI 3EF, UK; *and* 576 Fifth Avenue, #1103, New York, NY 10036

International Interfaith Centre, 2 Market Street, Oxford OXI 3EF UK

Interfaith Center of New York, 570 Lexington Avenue at 51st St., 22nd Floor, New York NY 10022 USA

Inter Faith Network for the UK, 5-7 Tavistock Pl., London WCIH 9SS UK

Inter Religious Federation for World Peace, 4 West, 43rd St. New York, NY 10036 USA

Multifaith Resources, c/o Rev. Charles White, PO Box 128, Wofford Heights, CA 93285 USA

North American Interfaith Network, c/o Dr. Peter Laurence, 512 Bedford Road, Armonk, NY 10504 USA

Peace Council, W. 9643 Rucks Rd., Cambridge, WI 53523 USA

Temple of Understanding, 570 Lexington Avenue at 51st St., 22nd Floor, New York NY 10022 USA   (Also see Interfaith Center of New York.)

World Conference on Religion and Peace (WCRP), WCRP/International, 777 UN Plaza, New York, NY 10017 USA

United Religions Initiative, PO BOX 29242, Presidio Building #1009, 1st Floor, San Franciso, CA 94129-0242 USA

World Congress of Faiths, 2 Market Street, Oxford OXI 3EF UK

World Faiths Encounter, 2 Market Street, Oxford OXI 3EF UK

Notes

1. Introduction, pp. 9–16

1. *The World's Parliament of Religions*, ed. John Henry Barrows, Chicago, 1893.

2. Details of writings on the 1893 Parliament are given in my *Pilgrimage of Hope*, SCM Press and Crossroads, 1992, pp. 323-5. *The Dawn of Religious Pluralism*, ed. by Richard Hughes Seager, Open Court, Illinois, 1993, has a useful introductory chapter and gives extracts from many of the addresses.

3. The 1933 Parliament is described in my *Inter-Faith Organizations, 1893-1979*, Edwin Mellen, Toronto 1980, pp. 167-170.

4. *Pilgrimage of Hope*, p. 299

5. See my *A Wider Vision*, Oneworld Publications, Oxford, 1996, p. 68.

6. *Pilgrimage of Hope*, p. 302

7. In Bede Griffiths, *Universal Wisdom*, Fount, HarperCollins, 1994, p. 43.

2. The Interfaith Movement, pp. 17–26

1. Hans Küng, *Global Responsibility*, Continnum, New York, and SCM Press 1991, p. 138.

2. For a fuller discussion of subjects and organizations covered in this chapter see *Pilgrimage of Hope*. For addresses, see Resources, above.

3. Globe-Trotting, pp. 27–41

1. *Visions of an Interfaith Future*, ed. Celia and David Storey, International Interfaith Centre, Oxford 1994, pp. 24-5.

2. See further *Pilgrimage of Hope*, pp. 270-8.

3. *Visions of an Interfaith Future*, p. 207

4. Ibid, p. 207

4. A New Age, pp. 42–52

1. Bede Griffiths, *A New Vision of Reality*, Collins, 1989, p. 9

2. For example, Ewart Cousins, *Christ of the Twenty First Century*, Continuum, New York, and Element, Shaftesbury, 1992.

3. Bede Griffiths, op cit, p. 19

4. Ibid, p. 20

5. Ibid, p. 20

6. Ibid, p. 48

7. Ibid, p. 281

8. Ibid, p. 91

9. Ibid, p. 282

10. Ibid, pp. 282-3

11. Ibid, pp. 282-3

12. Ibid

13. Bede Griffiths, *The Marriage of East and West*, Collins 1982.

14. Leonard Swidler, *The Meaning of Life at the Edge of the Third Millenium*, Paulist Press, 1992.

15. Hans Küng, *Global Responsibility*, Continuum, New York, and SCM Press, 1991 p. 3.

16. Ibid, p. 20.

17. Ibid, pp. 20-21.

18. Ibid, p. 22.

19. Niels C. Nielsen, Jr, *Fundamentalism, Mythos and World Religions*, State University of New York Press, Abany, 1993, p. viii.

5. Repentance, pp. 53-62

1. *The Times* 1.11.93, p. 2

2. *The Guardian* 19.3.93, p. 24

3. Ancient and Modern Revised No. 91

4. *Dialogue With a Difference*, ed. Tony Bayfield and Marcus Braybrooke, SCM Press 1992, see my chapter on "The Power of Suffering Love."

5. Quoted in *The Guardian* in an article by Tony Bartlett, 10.4.1991.

6. Brian Frost, *The Politics of Peace*, Darton, Longman and Todd 1991, p. viii.

7. A phrase used by Pope John Paul II at the World Day of Prayer for Peace at Assisi in 1986.

8. *Visions of an Interfaith Future*, ed. Celia and David Storey, op. cit, p. 35

9. *A Global Ethic*, op. cit.

10. Niels Nielsen, *Fundamentalismn, Mythos and World Religions*, State University of New York Press, Albany. 1993.

11. Quoted by Roger Hooker in *Belonging to Britain*, ed. Roger Hooker and John Sargent, CCBI, nd, p. 1

12. *Visions of an Interfaith Future*, p. 223

6. Theologies for a Pluralist World, pp. 63-72

1. George Carey, reported in *The Church Times*, 11.2.94, p. 2.

2. Robert Runcie in a sermon to General Synod of The Church of England, 9.7.89

3. Referred to by Rabbi Albert Friedlander in "Credo" in *The Times,* 5.3.94, p. 8.

4. Ibid.

5. Jonathan Sacks, "The Interfaith Imperative" in *Common Ground,* CCJ, 1990, No 1, pp. 10-13.

6. Jonathan Sacks, *The Persistence of Faith,* Weidenfeld and Nicolson, 1991, p.81.

7. Dawud O. S. Noibi, "O People of the Book: The Qur'an's Approach to Interfaith Cooperation." A paper given at the New Delhi Colloquium of the Inter-Religious Federation for World Peace, 1993.

8. John 14: 6. See Kenneth Cracknell, *Towards a New Relationship.* Epworth 1986, Chapter 5.

9. Cardinal Francis Arinze, "The Christian Commitment to Inter-religious Dialogue," L'Osservatore Romano, 17.7.89, para 3 and para 9.

10. John Hick, *God and the Universe of Faiths,* Macmillan 1973, Chapter 9.

11. M. Hilton and G. Marshall, *The Gospels and Rabbinic Judaism,* op cit., p. 154.

12. Kenneth Cragg in his Preface to *Readings in the Qur'an,* Collins, 1988, p.9.

13. George Appleton, "Faiths in Fellowship," World Faiths, No 101, Spring 1977, pp. 4-5.

14. "Religious Plurality, Theological Perspectives and Affirmations," Statement of the Baar Conference, 1990, reproduced in *Current Dialogue,* World Council of Churches, Geneva, No 19, January 1991, pp. 47-51.

15. H. B. Archbishop Anastasios of Tirana in *Current Dialogue,* WCC No 26, June 1994, p. 46.

16. Ibid, p. 47

17. *Multi-Faith Worship?,* Church Publishing House 1992, p. 36.

18. Pauline Webb, *Candles for Advent,* Collins Fount 1989.

19. See my Essex Hall Lecture 1993, "Interfaith Understanding and Co-operation: What are we afraid of?" Unitarian Information Department 1993.

20. Norman Solomon in *Dialogue with a Difference,* ed. Tony Bayfield and Marcus Braybrooke, SCM, 1992, pp. 147-8.

21. Stanley Samartha, *One Christ—Many Religions,* Orbis 1991, chap. 2, especially pp. 13-4.

22. For example the Prime Minister of India at 1993 Celebration Day in

New Delhi or the Queen's attendance at the Multi-Faith Act of Witness on Commonwealth day at Westminster Abbey.

7. Declaration Toward a Global Ethic, pp. 73-88

1. Quoted in Marcus Braybrooke, *Pilgrimage of Hope:* op cit., p. 13.
2. Ibid.
3. Ibid, p. 26
4. See *Stepping Stones to a Global Ethic,* ed. Marcus Braybrooke, SCM Press, London 1992; my paper was for the 1996 International Interfaith Centre Conference.
5. Hans Küng, *Global Responsibility: In Search of a New World Ethic.* Continuum, New York, and SCM Press, London 1991, p. 138. Subsequent references to this book are shown in the text as GR, followed by the page number. For a Chicago view of the process of preparing the text see "Moving Towards a Global Ethic," by Daniel Gómez-Ibáñez in *A SourceBook for Earth's Community of Religions,* ed. Joel Beversluis, CoNexus Press, Grand Rapids, Mich. 1995.
6. *A Global Ethic: A Declaration of the Parliament of the World's Religions,* ed. Hans Küng and Karl-Josef Kuschel, Continuum, New York, and SCM Press, London 1993, p. 47. Subsequent references to this book are shown in the text as GE, followed by the page number.
7. See above.
8. From the letter sent from participants in the Bangalore Workshop to the Chicago Parliament.
9. See *Stepping Stones to a Global Ethic,* ed. Marcus Braybrooke, Crossroad, New York, and SCM Press, London 1992, pp.116-119.
10. See *Visions of an Interfaith Future, op. cit. p. 137.*
11. Ibid, p. 138
12. Ibid, p. 137
13. Ibid, p. 135-6
14. Unpublished document, 5.11.93
15. Paul Waldau, "Beyond Praise of the Declaration of World Religions." An unpublished article.
16. Hans Küng, *A Global Ethic,* op. cit. p. 9.
17. Such work is being undertaken by the Global Ethic Foundation, the International Interfaith Centre, and others such as the Brahma Kumaris.

8. New Developments and a New Agenda, pp. 89–102

1. *Religion for Peace,* WCRP Newsletter, February 1995, p 3.
2. *World Faiths Encounter,* Number 16, March 1997, pp. 4-17. Marcus Braybrooke, *A Wider Vision,* Oneworld Publications 1996
3. *United Religions Journal,* Issue 3, Summer 1997, p. 3 .

4. Knitter, Paul, *One Earth, Many Religions,* Orbis 1996, p. 21.

5. Küng, Hans, *A Global Ethic for Global Politics and Economics,* SCM Press 1997.

6. Ellis, Marc, *Unholy Alliance,* SCM Press 1997.

7. Küng, Hans and Kuschel, Karl-Josef, *A Global Ethic,* Continuum, New York and SCM Press 1993, p. 9.

8. Choan-Seng Song, *The Compassionate God,* SCM Press 1982, pp. 259-60.

9. Global Theology, pp. 103–111

1. See above.

2. Jonathan Sacks, *The Interfaith Imperative.* op. cit.

3. Sarvepalli Radhakrishnan, *Religion and Society,* Kamala Lectures, Allen and Unwin 1947, p. 55.

4. Sarvepalli Radhakrishnan, *Religion in a Changing World,* Allen and Unwin 1967, p. 133.

5. Seshagiri Rao, *World Faiths Insight,* January 1983, New Series 6, p. 10.

6. Robert Runcie, *World Faiths Insight,* October 1986, New Series 14, p.14. The quotation from Paul Tillich is from *Christianity and the Encounter of World Religions,* Columbia University Press, New York and London 1963, p. 97.

7. See above p. 46, Leonard Swidler, *The Meaning of Life at the Edge of the Third Millenium,* op. cit. pp. 55-8.

8. Stanley Samartha, *One Christ, Many Religions,* Orbis 1991, p.4.

9. George Appleton, Sermon at King's College Chapel, London, 1970.

10. *Selections from Swami Vivekananda,* Advaita Ashram, Calcutta, 1957, p. 2.

11. Ibid, p. 5.

12. William Temple, *Nature, Man and God,* 1935, p. 322.

13. Tony Bayfield in *Dialogue with a Difference,* ed. Tony Bayfield and Marcus Braybrooke, SCM Press 1992, p. 21.

14. *Church Times,* 11.2.94.

15. Raimundo Panikkar, *The Vedic Experience,* Darton Longman and Todd 1977, p. 4.

16. Vivekananda, op cit., p.1.

17. Rabindranath Tagore. The quotation, without reference, is in *Theologizing in India,* ed. M. Amaladoss, T. K. Jon and G. Gispert-Sauch, Theological Publications in India, Bangalore 1981.

18. Wilfred Cantwell Smith, *Toward a World Theology,* Macmillan 1981.

19. John Hick, *Death and Eternal Life,* Collins 1976, p.27.

20. Sogyal Rinpoche, *The Tibetan Book of Living and Dying,* Rider 1992.

21. John Bowker, *Problems of Suffering in Religions of the World*, Cambridge University Press, 1970, p. 4.

22. *Dialogue with a Difference*, op. cit. pp. 81-93.

23. Quoted by J. Schoneveld in *The Quarterly Review*, Vol.4, No.4, Winter 1984 from Friedrich-Wilhelm Marquardt, *"Feinde um unsretwillen; Das judische Nein und die christliche Theologie,"* *Treue sur Thora, Beiträge zur Mitte des christlich-judischen Gesprächs; Festschrift fr Günther Harder zum 75 Geburtstag*, ed. Peter von der Osten-Sacken, Berlin, Institut Kirche und Judentum, 1979, p. 174.

24. Sarvepalli Radhakrishnan, *An Idealist View of Life*, George Allen and Unwin, 1932.

25. John 20:31

10. Global Spirituality, pp. 112–119

1. Kate Muir, "Near-death at W.H.Smith?" *The Times*, 16 August 1994.

2. Donald Nicholl, *Holiness*, Darton, Longman and Todd, 1981, p. 3.

3. Mahatma Gandhi in *Harijan*, quoted by Bede Griffiths in *Christian Ashram*, Darton, Longman and Todd, 1966, p. 127.

4. Quoted in Marcus Braybrooke, *Together to the Truth*, CLS, Madras, 1971, p. 139.

5. Quoted by Kenneth Leech in *The Social God*, Sheldon Press 1981, p. 42. See chapters 4 and 5.

6. See Marcus Braybrooke, *Together to the Truth*, CLS, Madras 1971, pp. 98-101.

7. Quoted in Ibid, p. 101.

8. Quoted in *Can We Pray Together?*, British Council of Churches, London 1983.

9. *The Oxford Book of Prayer*, ed. George Appleton, Oxford University Press, 1985; *The Lotus Prayer Book*, Integral Yoga Publications, Yogaville, Virginia 23921, 1986. Other examples are, *God of a Hundred Names*, ed. Barbara Greene and Victor Gollancz, Victor Gollancz, 1962, *Godspells,* John Prickett, The Book Guild, 1992, *Interpreted by Love*, ed. Elizabeth Basset, Darton, Longman and Todd, 1994.

10. Jonathan Sacks, *The Persistence of Faith*, Weidenfeld and Nicolson, 1991, p. 65.

11. Exodus 3:5.

11. One World Faith? pp. 120–132

1. Marcus Braybrooke, *Together to the Truth*, CLS, Madras and ISPCK, Delhi, 1971, p. 156.

2. *The World's Parliament of Religions*, ed. John Henry Barrows, The Parliament Publishing Co, Chicago, 1893, p. 1572.

3. J. H. Barrows, *Christianity: The World Religion*, A.C. McClurg, Chicago 1897, quoted by Richard Hughes Seager, *The World's Parliament of Religions*, Chicago, Illinois 1893: *America's Coming of Age*, Harvard University Doctoral Thesis, 1986, p. 238

4. Sarvepalli Radhakrishnan, *Eastern Religions and Western Thought*, Oxford University Press 1939, pp. viii-ix.

5. Prince Philip, Preface to Küng, *Global Responsibility*, SCM Press, 1990.

6. See above Chap. 9.

7. See Marcus Braybrooke, *Pilgrimage of Hope*.

8. A Global Ethic, eds Hans Küng and Karl-Josef Kuschel, SCM Press, 1993.

9. S. J. Samartha, *One Christ–Many Religions*, Orbis, New York 1991, p. 4.

10. Durwood Foster, "The Quest for a Universal Ultimology" in *Visions of an Interfaith Future*, ed. David and Celia Storey, International Interfaith Centre, Oxford, 1994, p. 158.

11. Ibid.

12. Raimundo Panikkar in *The Myth of Christian Uniqueness*, see note 7, p. 109.

13. Ibid.

14. Ibid, p. 110.

15. Masao Abe in *Visions of an Interfaith Future*, op.cit., pp.164-5.

16. Bede Griffiths, *A New Vision of Reality*, Collins 1989, p. 287.

17. Ibid, p. 293.

18. Ibid, p. 294.

19. Ibid, p. 296.

20. Paul F Knitter, *No Other Name*, SCM Press 1985, p. 231. See also Paul F. Knitter, *Jesus and the Other Names*, Orbis 1996.

21. Ibid.

22. Philippians 2:7-8.

23. Hans Ucko, *Common Roots: New Horizons*, WCC Geneva 1994, p. 84.

24. Durwood Foster, see note 10, p. 160.

25. Quoted by Hans Küng, *Judaism*, SCM Press 1991, p. 258.

26. Quoted by Zaki Badawi, *World Faiths Insight*, June 1986, p. 11.

27. John Hick, *God and the Universe of Faiths*, Macmillan 1973, p. 147.

28. A song "World in Union" by Gustav Holst and Charlie Skarbek, Standard Music Ltd, London, 1991.

29. Emma Segret Perez in *Visions of a Better World*, Brahma Kumaris World Spiritual University, 1993, p.132.

Comments on *Faith and Interfaith in a Global Age*

"One can only be grateful that Marcus Braybrooke has shared his breadth of experience in this sensitive reflection on global interfaith activity. His chapter on 'Repentance' is particularly compelling because it redresses a tendency in many interfaith circles to speak only of the highest ideals of each tradition of faith. He is right to suggest that activities enabling participants to share the suffering caused or ignored by their communities of faith are essential in realizing the interfaith vision." —Dr. Robert Traer,
Director, International Association for Religious Freedom

"Amid the hostilities of religions and the competition among interfaith efforts, one person stands out as a source of fair judgement, sound scholarship, and supportive friendship for all. Marcus Braybrooke is that person. So when he adds new words about the world of faiths, it is wise to pay heed." —The Rev. William E. Swing,
Bishop of California and Chair, United Religions Initiative

"Within this volume are the seeds of deep reflection and creative action. Of particular value is the section on 'A New Age,' which outlines the way we look at religious truths. Braybrooke does not ignore the unsettling concern of many who fear the watering-down of their own beliefs if they attempt to enter into the faith worlds of others. He stands firmly in this position: 'I feel it is rootedness that gives the security of openness. My meeting with those of other faiths has been as a disciple of Jesus Christ.' "
—Marian Bohen, in *Journal of Ecumenical Studies*

The Rev. **MARCUS BRAYBROOKE**, M.A., M.Phil., is an Anglican priest who has served as a central figure in the interfaith movement for thirty years. His contributions include: Director of the Council of Christians and Jews; co-editor of the journal *World Faiths Insight;* past Chairman and now Joint President of the World Congress of Faiths; key participant in the International Interfaith Centre at Oxford; Trustee of the Council for a Parliament of the World's Religions and of the Peace Council; author of *Pilgrimage of Hope: One Hundred Years of Global Interfaith Dialogue,* and other books.